English for Presentations

Marion Grussendorf

SHORT COURSE
SERIES

Verfasserin	Marion Grussendorf, Köln
kritische Durchsicht	Charles La Fond, Wien
	Louise Kennedy, Hamburg
Verlagsredaktion	Janan Barksdale
Redaktionelle Mitarbeit	Christine House, Oliver Busch (Wortliste), Sylee Gore, Elizabeth Hine, Louise Kennedy
Bildredaktion	Uta Hübner, Gertha Maly
Gesamtgestaltung und technische Umsetzung	Sylvia Lang

Bildquellen

Titelfoto: Fotosearch/Bananastock
Fotos: Corbis GmbH: S. 6/D. Cooper-zefa, S. 13/P. Winbladh-zefa, S. 17/J. Henley, S. 20/G. Schuster-zefa, S. 29/W. Morgan; Getty Images: S. 5/PM Images/K. Moskowitz, S. Schauer, S. 10, S. 19/T. Prasse, S. 38, S. 40, S. 44, S. 48/H. Grey, S. 50/R. Estakhrian, S. 53; Zefa: S. 24/masterfile, S. 26/L. Williams, S. 31/L. Williams (4)/J. Pelaez/E. Rian, S.34/masterfile H. Vu, S. 42/masterfile N. Hendrickson, S. 49/H. Schneider, S. 57/masterfile J. Feingersh; Fotosearch/Bananastock: S. 59
Symbole: Andreas Terglane, Kassel
Cartoons und Illustrationen: Oxford Designers and Illustrators

Tonaufnahmen

Aufnahmestudio: Nordquist Productions, Berlin
Aufnahmeleitung: Johan Nordquist, Janan Barksdale
Toningenieur: Olaf Stemme
Sprecher: Syd Atlas, Laura Cameron, Marianne Graffon, Shaun Lawton, Clayton Nemrow, Ben Posener

Weitere Titel in der *Short Course Series*:

English for Accounting	Bestell-Nr. 18806
English for the Automobile Industry	Bestell-Nr. 18776
English for Customer Care	Bestell-Nr. 18822
English for Emails	Bestell-Nr. 18784
English for Human Resources	Bestell-Nr. 18814
English for Marketing and Advertising	Bestell-Nr. 18768
English for Meetings	Bestell-Nr. 18741
English for Telephoning	Bestell-Nr. 18733

 http://www.cornelsen.de

1. Auflage, 1. Druck 2005

Alle Drucke dieser Auflage sind inhaltlich unverändert und können im Unterricht nebeneinander verwendet werden.

© 2005 Cornelsen Verlag, Berlin

Druck: CS-Druck CornelsenStürtz, Berlin

ISBN 3-464-01875-X

Bestellnummer 18750

 Gedruckt auf säurefreiem Papier,
umweltschonend hergestellt aus chlorfrei gebleichten Faserstoffen.

Inhalt

PAGE	UNIT TITLE	TOPICS	USEFUL PHRASES
5	**1 Let's get started**	Welcoming your audience Introducing yourself and the topic Dealing with nervousness	Opening a presentation Structuring a presentation Organizational details (talking about timing, handouts, questions) Ways to get the audience's attention
15	**2 Today's topic is …**	Body language Tips on presenting to an English-speaking audience	Signposting (phrases to organize your presentation) Talking about difficult issues Referring to other points Adding ideas
23	**3 My next slide shows …**	Presentation tools Using approximate numbers Creating effective visuals Presenting visuals effectively	Introducing visuals Saying numbers The rule of six Making contrasts and describing results Emphasizing important points
32	**4 As you can see from this graph …**	Types of visuals Describing graphs and charts Interpreting visuals Tips for describing trends	Talking about visuals Talking about trends (verb tenses, adjectives and adverbs)
42	**5 To sum up …**	Concluding a presentation Strategies for a good conclusion	Summarizing the main points Making recommendations Phrases for effective conclusions Using your voice effectively (stressing words, making pauses)
50	**6 Any questions?**	Handling the question and answer session Dealing with interruptions	Dealing with questions Asking polite questions Anticipating questions Reformulating questions

PAGE	APPENDIX
58	**Test yourself!**
60	**Answer key**
66	**Transcripts**
70	**A–Z word list**
73	**Presentation trainer**
78	**Useful phrases and vocabulary**

Vorwort

Präsentationen gehören heute in vielen Firmen und Arbeitsbereichen zum Berufsalltag. Immer häufiger wird es dabei notwendig, auch auf Englisch zu präsentieren. Doch selbst Arbeitnehmern mit guten Sprachkenntnissen erscheint eine Präsentation in der Fremdsprache oft als große Herausforderung. Mit **English for Presentations** lernen Sie gezielt die Redewendungen und Vokabeln, die Sie für Ihre Präsentation brauchen. Gleichzeitig erhalten Sie nützliche Tipps, wie Sie sicher und effektiv auf Englisch präsentieren.

English for Presentations umfasst sechs Units, die alle relevanten Themenfelder und Teile einer Präsentation behandeln. Jede Unit beginnt mit dem so genannten First of all, das aus kurzen Übungen, einem Fragebogen oder Quiz besteht. Es folgen zahlreiche Auszüge aus Präsentationen mit Hörtexten (auf der beiliegenden Audio-CD), Lückentexten sowie eine Vielfalt von anderen Übungen. So können Sie Ihr Wissen überprüfen, neue Redewendungen lernen oder bestimmte Strukturen üben. Useful Phrases-Kästchen vermitteln gebräuchliche Formulierungen und Tipps für Ihre Präsentation. Gegen Ende jeder Unit fasst eine Checklist die wichtigsten Punkte zusammen. Ein abschließender Summing up-Text, der sich inhaltlich auf das Thema der Unit bezieht, soll zur Diskussion anregen.

English for Presentations behandelt nicht nur die sprachlichen Fertigkeiten, sondern auch Präsentationstechniken, Aufbau, Struktur und Darbietung einer Präsentation. Dabei geht es unter anderem um Körpersprache, Visualisierung und Interaktion mit dem Publikum. Wenn alle Units bearbeitet sind, können Sie Ihren Kenntnisstand anhand eines Kreuzworträtsels überprüfen – Test yourself!

Im Anhang von **English for Presentations** finden Sie den praktischen Presentation Trainer. Der Presentation Trainer ermöglicht es Ihnen, sich optimal auf jede Präsentation vorzubereiten, sie zu strukturieren und anschließend zu bewerten. Wenn Sie den Presentation Trainer jeweils kopieren, können Sie alle relevanten Schritte und Fragen systematisch durchgehen und eintragen. Damit sind Sie bestens für Ihre Präsentation gerüstet.

Der Anhang enthält darüber hinaus einen Answer key, mit dem Sie Ihre Antworten selbstständig überprüfen können sowie eine A–Z word list. Im Teil Useful phrases and vocabulary können Sie auch am Arbeitsplatz nützliche Redewendungen und Begriffe nachschlagen, die Sie für eine englischsprachige Präsentation benötigen.

Let's get started ...

**Work with a partner. Ask the questions below and make a note of the answers.
Then tell the group what you found out and discuss.**

❶ How often do you give presentations in your job?

❷ Who do you normally present to? (Colleagues, customers, other firms, etc)

❸ When was the last time you gave a presentation in English? Was it a success? If yes, why? If not, why not? Explain your answer.

❹ How do you feel about presenting in a foreign language?

❺ Think of an excellent (or terrible) presentation that you have attended. What made it good (or bad)?

2–4

1 **Listen to the opening sentences of the three presentations and complete the table.**

	Presentation 1	Presentation 2	Presentation 3
Presenter's name			
Presenter's position / function			
Topic of presentation			
Who is the presentation for?			

Which presentations are formal and which are less formal?

VOCABULARY ASSISTANT

to access *zugreifen auf*   to appreciate *zu schätzen wissen*
to dedicate *widmen*   to evaluate *bewerten, einstufen*
shelving system *Regalsystem*   at short notice *kurzfristig*

2 Listen to the openings again and complete the sentences.

2

Presentation 1

1 _____ , let me thank you all for being here today.

2 Let me _____ myself. My name is ...

3 I'm here today to _____ our new semi-automatic shelving system.

4 My talk is _____ relevant to those of you who _____ for the different parts we supply.

Presentation 2

3

5 I'm happy that so many of you could _____ today at such short

_____ .

6 As you can see on the _____ , our _____ today is project documentation.

7 This is extremely _____ for all of us who are directly _____ in international project management, right?

Presentation 3

4

8 I'm _____ that you all have very tight _____ , so I appreciate you taking the time to come here today.

9 As you _____ know, my name is ... . I'm the new _____ manager here at Weston Ltd.

10 Today's topic will be very important for you as _____ since _____ your help to evaluate and select candidates for training.

3 Put the sentences from above in the correct category (a–d).

a saying what the topic is: _____

b welcoming the audience: _____

c saying who you are: *2,* _____

d saying why the topic is relevant for the audience: _____

Now put a–d in the order you would use to start a presentation.

4 **Match these less formal phrases with the more formal phrases in the table.**

What I want to do today is ...

I know you are all very busy ...

As you know, I'm ...

OK, shall we get started?

It's good to see you all here.

Hi, everyone.

Today I'm going to talk about ...

In my talk I'll tell you about ...

More formal	Less formal
Good afternoon, ladies and gentlemen.	1
Today I would like to ...	2
Let me just start by introducing myself. My name is ...	3
It's a pleasure to welcome you today.	4
In my presentation I would like to report on ...	5
The topic of today's presentation is ...	6
I suggest that we begin now.	7
I'm aware that you all have very tight schedules ...	8

5 **Now practise the opening of a presentation. Use phrases from the box and follow the flow chart.**

welcome audience → introduce yourself → introduce topic → say why audience will be interested

---

THE OPENING OF A PRESENTATION

Welcoming the audience
Good morning/afternoon, ladies and gentlemen.
Hello/Hi everyone.
First of all, let me thank you all for coming here today.
I'm happy/delighted that so many of you could make it today.

Introducing yourself
Let me introduce myself. I'm Dave Elwood from ...
For those of you who don't know me, my name is ...
As you probably know, I'm the new HR manager.
I'm head of logistics here at Air Spares.
I'm here in my function as the Head of Controlling.

Introducing your topic
As you can see on the screen, our topic today is ...
Today's topic is ...
What I'd like to present to you today is ...
The subject of my presentation is ...

Saying why your topic is relevant for your audience
My talk is particularly relevant to those of you/us who ...
Today's topic is of particular interest to those of you/us who ...
My/The topic is very important for you because ...
By the end of this talk you will be familiar with ...

! Remember to use words like 'we', 'us' and 'our' to highlight common interest.

STRUCTURING A PRESENTATION (I)

Most formal – and many informal – presentations have three main parts and follow this simple formula:

1 Tell the audience what you are going to say! = Introduction
2 Say it!   = Main part
3 Tell them what you said!   = Conclusion

There are several ways you can tell the audience what you are going to say.

would like + infinitive
Today **I'd like to tell** you about our new plans.
This morning **I'd like to bring** you up-to-date on our department.

going to + infinitive
I'm going to talk to you today new developments in the R & D Department.
This afternoon **I'm going to be reporting** on the new division.

will + infinitive
I'll begin by explaining the function.
I'll start off by reviewing our progress.
After that, **I'll move** on to my next point.

will be + verb -ing
I'll be talking about our guidelines for Internet use.
During the next hour we**'ll be looking** at the advantages of this system.

---

6 **Complete the sentences with the correct form of the verb and a sentence ending from below.**

you on the proposed training project

you up to date on SEKO's investment plans

you how the database works

~~you an overview of our present market position~~

at business opportunities in Asia

on our financial targets for the division

by telling you about what Jane's group is working on

about EU tax reform

1 give   Today I'd like to _give you an overview of our present market position._ _____
2 show   I'll be _showing_ _____
3 talk   During the next two hours we'll be _____
4 bring   I'd like to _____
5 report   This afternoon I'm going to _____
6 update   Today I'd like to _____
7 look   This morning we'll be _____
8 begin   Today I'll _____

> **STRUCTURING A PRESENTATION (II)**
>
> The purpose of the introduction is not only to tell the audience who you are, what the talk is about and why it is relevant to them, you also want to tell the audience (briefly) how the talk is structured. Here are some useful phrases to talk about the structure.
>
> **I've divided** my presentation **into** three (main) parts: x, y and z.
> In my presentation **I'll focus on** three major issues.
> **First (of all)**, I'll be looking at ..., **second** ..., and **third** ...
> **I'll begin/start off by** explaining ...
> **Then/Next/After that**, I'll go on to ...
> **Finally**, I'll offer some solutions.
>
> **!** The most common way to structure a presentation is to have three main parts, and then subdivide them into (three) smaller sections.

7 **Complete the gaps with the words below.**

> after • all • areas • divided • finally • start • then • third

1

I'll be talking to you today about the after-sales service plans we offer. I'll _____ ¹ by describing the various packages in detail. _____ ² I'll go on to show you some case studies. _____ ³, I'll discuss how you can choose the best plan to meet your customers' needs.

2

I've _____ ⁴ my talk into three main parts. First of _____ ⁵, I'll tell you something about the history of our company. _____ ⁶ that I'll describe how the company is structured and finally, I'll give you some details about our range of products and services.

3

I'd like to update you on what we've been working on over the last year. I'll focus on three main _____ ⁷: first, our joint venture in Asia; second, the new plant in Charleston. And _____ ⁸, our redevelopment project.

8 **Complete the sentences with the correct prepositions.**

> about • at • for • into • of • on • to • with

1 Thank you _____ coming all this way.

2 I've divided my presentation _____ three parts.

3 First of all, I'll give you an overview _____ our financial situation.

4 First, we'll be looking _____ the company's sales in the last two quarters.

5 In the first part of my presentation I'll focus _____ the current project status.

6 Point one deals _____ APG's new regulations for Internet use.

7 Secondly, I'll talk _____ our investment in office technology.

8 After that I'll move on _____ the next point.

5

9 The project manager of a German construction company is giving a presentation to his colleagues. Put the sentences in the right order. Then listen and check.

☐ a This morning I'd like to update you on the current status of work at the construction site. The information I give you today should help you with planning your next steps.

☐ b For those of you who don't know me, my name is Gordon Selfridge. Let me just write that down for you. OK. I'm the project manager in charge of the Bak Tower building project in Dubai.

☐ c I've divided my presentation into three parts.

☐1☐ d Hello, everyone.

☐ e Then I'll move on to the problems we're facing with our local suppliers.

☐ f First of all, let me thank you for coming here today. I'm aware that you're all busy preparing for the annual meeting this week, so I really appreciate you taking the time to be here.

☐ g I'll start off by showing you some photos of the building site and discussing the progress we've made since January.

☐ h My talk should take about 30 minutes. Please feel free to interrupt me at any time with questions.

☐ i I'll end with some ideas for reducing labour costs that we've been looking into.

☐ j Oh, and don't worry about taking notes. I'll be handing out copies of the PowerPoint slides at the end of my talk.

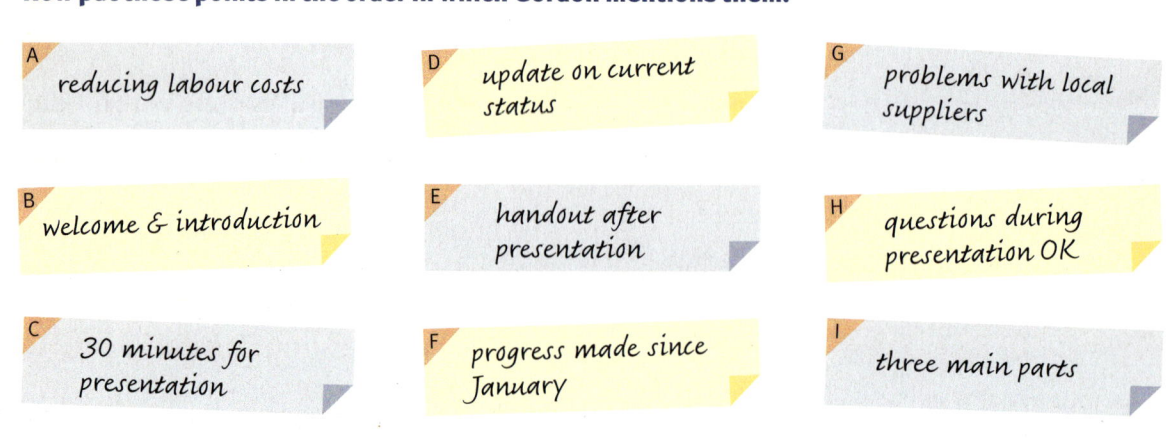

| **VOCABULARY ASSISTANT** | current status *aktueller Stand*
 to face *konfrontiert sein mit*
 progress *Fortschritt*   supplier *Lieferant* |

Now put these points in the order in which Gordon mentions them.

A reducing labour costs

D update on current status

G problems with local suppliers

B welcome & introduction

E handout after presentation

H questions during presentation OK

C 30 minutes for presentation

F progress made since January

I three main parts

10 **Look again at these sentences from the presentation and replace the highlighted words with words or phrases from the box below.**

after that • ~~begin~~ • I'm • realize • responsible for • sections • turn

1 I'll start off by showing you ... *I'll begin by showing you ...* _____

2 I've divided my presentation into three parts. _____

3 For those of you who don't know me, my name is Gordon Smith. _____
_____

4 Then I'll move on to the problems ... _____
_____

5 I'm the project manager in charge of our Dubai building project. _____
_____

6 I'm aware that you're all busy preparing for the annual meeting ... _____
_____

ORGANIZATION

The final part of the introduction deals with the organization of the talk: how long it will last, whether there will be handouts and how questions will be handled.

Timing
My presentation will take about 20 minutes.
It should take about 30 minutes to cover these issues.

Handouts
Does everybody have a handout / brochure / report? Please take one, and pass them on.
Don't worry about taking notes. I've put all the important statistics on a handout for you.
I'll be handing out copies of the PowerPoint slides at the end of my talk.
I'll email the PowerPoint presentation to you.

Questions
There will be time for questions after my presentation.
If you have any questions, feel free to interrupt me at any time.
Feel free to ask questions at any time during my talk.

---

11 **Match sentence parts from each column to make typical sentences from the introduction.**

1 For those of you who don't know me,   a to take notes. Everything is on the handout.
2 Feel free to   b about 10 minutes.
3 This won't take more   c I'm Bob Kay in charge of the software division.
4 I'll be passing out   d ask questions at any time.
5 This part of the presentation will take e for questions after my talk.
6 I'll start off by giving you   f an overview of our product range.
7 There's no need   g handouts in a few minutes.
8 There will be time   h than 20 minutes of your time.

12 **Listen to the beginnings of four presentations. Which one starts with …**

6–9

a a rhetorical question? ☐
b an interesting fact? ☐
c an anecdote? ☐
d a problem to think about? ☐

Listen again and complete the sentences.

1 _____ , I was sitting in the waiting room at the dentist's the other day and I _____ something very interesting in one of the _____ that was lying there.

2 _____ you worked in a small to medium-sized company and were _____ for making people in your company aware of health and safety issues. How would you _____ ?

3 _____ that the number of possible ways of playing the first four moves per side in a game of chess is …?

4 So, let me start by _____ . Why should we introduce a double quality check here at Auto Spares & Parts …? Well, I'm here today to _____ .

GETTING THE AUDIENCE'S ATTENTION

Experts say that the first few minutes of a presentation are the most important. If you are able to get the audience's attention quickly, they will be interested in what you have to say. Here are a few techniques you can use to start your talk.

Ask a rhetorical question
Is market research important for brand
  development?
Do we really need quality assurance?

Tell them a story or anecdote
I remember when I attended a meeting in Paris. …
At a conference in Madrid, I was once asked the
  following question: …

Start with an interesting fact
According to an article I read recently, central banks
  are now buying euros instead of dollars.
Did you know that fast food consumption has
  increased by 600% in Europe since 2002?

Give them a problem to think about
Suppose you wanted to set up a new call centre.
  How would you go about it?
Imagine you had to reorganize the sales
  department. What would be your first step?

---

13 **Match items from the three columns to make attention-grabbing openings.**

1 Did you know that	that 'can't is a four-letter word.	Who would you tell first?
2 I read in an article somewhere	compete with the Chinese?	by eliminating one olive from each salad served in first-class?
3 Imagine	American Airlines saved $40,000 in 1987	Of course we can!
4 Can we really	you won a million euros.	I tend to agree with that!

What presentation topics could you use each of the openings above for? Choose one of the openings and use it to practise the introduction of a talk.

14   Translate these sentences. Try to use expressions from this unit.

1   Gut, lassen Sie uns anfangen.
2   Das Thema meiner heutigen Präsentation ist Kundenzufriedenheit.
3   Meine Präsentation wird etwa eine halbe Stunde dauern.
4   Ich konzentriere mich auf drei Punkte.
5   Als erstes werden wir uns den aktuellen Projektstatus anschauen.
6   Wussten Sie, dass dieses Auto in China sehr beliebt ist?

15   Put the notes in the correct order, then prepare two openings of a presentation: a formal one and a less formal one. Use the checklist for introductions below if you need help.

a   B. Müller, product manager, FIT-Healthcare

b   20 minutes

f   promotional video

Good morning, ladies and gentlemen.

c   relevant for sales staff

g   three parts

Hi, everyone.

d   products

h   new wellness products

e   questions at end

i   welcome, etc

CHECKLIST FOR INTRODUCTIONS

☑   1   Welcome the audience.
☑   2   Introduce yourself (name, position/function).
☑   3   State your topic.
☑   4   Say why your topic is important for the audience.
☑   5   Describe the structure of your talk (what issues, points, etc are covered and when you will be dealing with them).
☑   6   Talk about the organization (timing, handouts, questions).

16   Now it's your turn. Think of a talk you have given or would like to give and use the checklist to prepare your introduction. Try to use phrases from this unit.

Read this article from a website on business communication and discuss the questions which follow.

Dealing with nervousness

The American author Mark Twain once put it like this: "There are two types of people: those that are nervous and those that are liars." So, once you accept that (almost) everybody who gives a presentation – whether formal or informal, long or short, to strangers or colleagues – is nervous, then you just need to find ways to deal with nervousness and even learn how to use it to your advantage.

Let's first look at ways to deal with and reduce nervousness.

1 **Prepare well.** "Failing to prepare is preparing to fail." Preparation is the key to a successful presentation. Nothing will relax you more than knowing exactly what you want to say and having practised saying it. Make sure you practise your talk until you feel at home with it – then you can concentrate on other things.

2 **Learn to relax.** Doing stretching or breathing exercises before your talk can help you to reduce nervousness. One example: before your presentation, sit comfortably with your back straight. Breathe in slowly, hold your breath for about five seconds, then slowly exhale. You can relax your facial muscles by opening your eyes and mouth wide, then closing them tightly.

3 **Check out the room.** Make yourself familiar with the place where you will be speaking. Arrive early, walk around the room and make sure everything you need for your talk is there. Practise using any equipment (eg microphone, video projector, OHP) you plan to work with.

4 **Know your audience.** If possible, greet your audience as they arrive and chat with them. It will be easier to speak to people who are not complete strangers.

Visualize success

5 **Concentrate on the message.** Try to focus on the message and your audience – not on your own fears.

6 **Visualize success.** Imagine yourself speaking to your audience in a loud and clear voice. Then visualize the audience applauding loudly at the end of your talk as you smile.

Use the steps above to reduce nervousness, but also remember that being nervous isn't all bad. Many experienced presenters say that you can also use your nervousness to give you that extra energy that you need to give a good performance.

Over to you

What other tips can you think of for dealing with nervousness?
How do you deal with nervousness before or during a presentation?
How do you prepare your presentations?

2

Today's topic is …

Do this quiz about body language. Sometimes more than one answer is possible.

YOU'RE GIVING A PRESENTATION …

1 How should you stand?
a Arms crossed on chest.
b Straight but relaxed.
c Knees unlocked.

2 What should you do with your hands?
a Put hands on hips.
b Put one hand in a pocket.
c Keep hands by your side.

3 How can you emphasize something?
a Point finger at the audience.
b Move or lean forward to show that something is important.
c Use a pointer to draw attention to important facts.

4 What should you do when you feel nervous?
a Hold a pen or cards in your hands.
b Walk back and forth.
c Look at the flip chart or screen (not at the audience).

5 How should you keep eye contact with the audience?
a Make eye contact with each individual often.
b Choose some individuals and look at them as often as possible.
c Spread attention around the audience.

6 How fast should you speak?
a About 20% more slowly than normal.
b Just as fast as in a normal conversation.
c Faster than in a normal conversation.

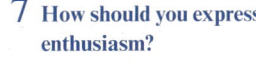

7 How should you express enthusiasm?
a By raising voice level.
b By waving arms.
c By making hand or arm gestures for important points.

Discuss your answers with a partner. How much do you think personality and culture influence your body language during a presentation?

10–13

1 Listen to these excerpts from four different presentations. Write the number of the presentation next to the topic.

short-time work ☐   insurance market ☐   handbooks ☐   transport regulations ☐

Now decide in which presentation(s) the presenter is …

- informing the audience about something: _____
- suggesting some solutions to a problem: _____

2   **Listen again to how the presenters talk about the purpose of their talks and complete the gaps.**

10–13

1   What _____ today is to make some suggestions on how we can make our handbooks more user-friendly.

2   The _____ of my talk is to provide you with information on the _____ in the insurance market in the last few months.

3   What I _____ this morning is to show you how we could reorganize our working hours.

4   The _____ is to bring you up to date with the latest changes which will be introduced on January 1.

3   **Use the notes to write sentences which can be used to state the purpose of a presentation. (Put in prepositions and other words where necessary.)**

1   purpose of talk today/update you/new developments/R&D

_____

_____

2   what I want to do/present alternatives/existing booking procedures

_____

_____

3   my aim/show/how cut costs/IT support

_____

4   objective of presentation/give overview/British job market

_____

_____

5   our goal/determine/sales targets/next year

_____

6   here today/report/company's investment plans

_____

4   **A team of German traffic experts is visiting the Belgian 'Traffic Support Centre', which uses state-of-the-art technology and new methods for traffic control. Peter van Heugen, a representative from the TSC, is giving a presentation on the centre's activities. Listen to this excerpt and say in what order the following points are mentioned.**

14

☐ a   what the TSC does (main activities)

☐ b   how traffic data is collected

☐ c   why the TSC was started

☐ d   how motorists benefit from the system

☐ e   how traffic information is given to motorists

14

Now listen to the presentation again and complete the gaps.

OK, _____1 the background and the reason we developed the programme.
Any questions? OK. So, _____2 to the next point and take a closer look at
the Traffic Support Centre itself. _____3, the TSC was set up in 2001 to help
traffic flow more smoothly and basically to make the lives of motorists easier. In this part of my
presentation _____4 you about the centre's activities, how we work exactly and
how motorists benefit from our services.

So _____5 a brief overview of
the TSC's activities. Our main activities are to collect, analyze
and communicate traffic information. After collecting traffic
data from a number of different sources we analyze them
and then we inform the media, the police or other
authorities, and – last but not least – the motorists. (…)

This now leads us to _____6. How
does the TSC collect data? Traffic monitoring equipment has
been installed across the main traffic routes, which helps us
gather real-time information on traffic speed and traffic flow. Additionally, we use variable traffic
sensors and cameras. We also work together with other partners and authorities, for example the
police, traffic officers and the media. Let me show you a few examples of how this works. (…)
_____7 collecting data.

_____8 to the next issue. How do we communicate information to motorists?
We do this in a number of ways: by using electronic road signs, the Internet and radio and state-of-
the-art telephone technology. (…)

Let me now come back to _____9. The TSC wants to make the lives of
motorists easier. So, in what ways does the motorist benefit? Well, … first: through real-time
information about the traffic situation. Second, through better advice about alternative routes.
Third, through safer roads and less driver stress.

| **VOCABULARY ASSISTANT** | to gather *sammeln*
monitoring equipment *Überwachungsgeräte*
variable *beweglich* |

5 'Signposting' phrases are used to help guide the audience through a presentation.
Complete this box of useful phrases with highlighted phrases from the presentation in exercise 4.

SIGNPOSTING

Saying what is coming

1   *In this part of my presentation, I'd like to tell you about …*

2   _____

Moving on to the next point

This leads directly to the next part of my talk.

3   _____

4   _____

5   _____

Indicating the end of a section

This brings me to the end of my second point.

6   _____

7   _____

Referring back

As I mentioned before, …

8   _____

Let's go back to what we were discussing earlier.

9   _____

Summarizing a point

I'd like to sum up the main points.

Let me briefly summarize what I've said so far.

---

6 Make 'signpost' sentences using elements from each column.

1 Before I move on to my next point,	come back to	next question.
2 This brings	the issue	point, which is price.
3 This leads	let me go	this question later.
4 Let's now turn to	we were discussing	our new sales strategies.
5 As I mentioned	to the next	a brief overview of our activities.
6 I'd like to	before, I'd like to give you	earlier.
7 Let's go back to what	us directly to my	through the main issues once more.
8 As I said earlier,	I'll be focussing on	of customer service.

7 **Complete the sentences with words from the box.**

> back • covered • discussing • inform • leads • main points • sum up • wanted

1 Let me now summarize the _____ .

2 We will be _____ our sales targets today.

3 In my talk I'll _____ you about new marketing techniques.

4 Before I move on, let me just _____ what I've said so far.

5 I think we have _____ everything for today.

6 OK, that's all I _____ to say about time management.

7 This _____ directly to my second point.

8 Let's go _____ to what I said at the beginning of my presentation.

8 **Complete the sentences using expressions with 'as' and the information in the notes. Add missing words where necessary.**

> **EXPRESSIONS WITH 'AS'**
>
> As you all know, …
> As I've already explained, …
> As I mentioned before/earlier, …
> As I pointed out in the first section, …
> As you can see, …

1 we/no budget for new software/this year (I mentioned this before)

   As I mentioned before, we have no budget for new software this year.

2 Tony Dale/new marketing manager/print media (you all know this already)

   _____

3 can't operate from local airport/because no permission (I said this at the beginning of my talk)

   _____

4 choose between two options (I explained this ten minutes ago)

   _____

5 sales have increased/10% since beginning of year (you can see this on the slide)

   _____

15

9 **Marta Pfeiffer is updating her group on some problems they've been having with one of the company's product lines. Listen to this excerpt from her informal presentation and say whether the following statements are true or false.**

1 The company is having problems with their new men's cosmetic products.

2 The problems are in three areas: supply, distribution and production.

3 Marta identifies two problems in the area of supply: the plastic bottle supplier can't deliver the quantity they need and the quality of the bottles is poor.

4 They have had to return around 14% of the bottles.

5 They have to take care of the supply problem soon or they'll have trouble with Father's Day sales.

10   **Complete these sentences from the presentation with the correct form of verbs from the list. Then listen again to check.**

15

> accept • cope • deal • have • identify • prevent • run • solve

As you probably know, we _____ currently _____¹ difficulties with our new men's cosmetic line.

I'd like to quickly _____² the problems and then make some suggestions on how we can _____³ with the consequences.

We've been trying to _____⁴ with these problems – the delays, the poor quality – all along, but so far we've not been able to find ways to _____⁵ them from happening again.

If we _____⁷ (not) our supply problems within the next two weeks, we _____⁸ into serious trouble with respect to our Christmas business.

It's clear we can no longer continue to _____⁶ these conditions.

TALKING ABOUT (DIFFICULT) ISSUES

I think we first need to **identify** the problem.
Of course we'll have to **clarify** a few points before we start.
We will have to **deal with** the problem of increasing prices.
How shall we **cope with** unfair business practices?
The question is: why don't we **tackle** the distribution problems?
If we don't **solve** this problem now, we'll get into serious trouble soon.
We will have to **take care of** this problem now.

REFERRING TO OTHER POINTS

I'd like to mention some critical points **in connection with / concerning** payment.
There are a few problems **regarding** the quality.
With respect / regard to prices, we need more details.
According to the survey, our customers are unhappy with this product.

ADDING IDEAS

In addition to this, I'd like to say that our IT business is going very well.
Moreover / Furthermore, there are other interesting facts we should take a look at.
As well as that, we can offer excellent conditions.
Apart from being too expensive, this model is also too big.
To increase sales we need a new strategy **plus** more people.

11 **Choose the correct verb to fit the sentence.**

1   How are we going to solve / deal / tackle with delivery problems?

2   I don't think we can cope / tackle / take care with fewer people.

3   We think it's important to identify / deal / cope the problems now.

4   Who will take care / deal / tackle of our business clients?

5   We have been trying to cope / solve / take care the software problem.

6   Before we go on, let's identify / clarify / solve this question.

12 **Complete the sentences with the words from the box.**

according to • apart from • concerns • moreover • regarding • with regard

1   I'll give you an overview of some figures _____ to car exports.

2   _____ , I'd like to tell you something about the new software.

3   Let's now turn to the next question which _____ customer service.

4   _____ a few spelling mistakes, the new brochure is very good.

5   Let me give you some details _____ our Chinese factory.

6   _____ the handbook, the scanner is user-friendly.

13 **Translate these sentences. Try to use expressions from this unit.**

1   Lassen Sie uns jetzt zum nächsten Punkt gehen.

2   Wie Sie alle wissen, ist unser heutiges Thema die Globalisierung.

3   Mein Ziel ist es, Sie über die neusten Entwicklungen zu informieren.

4   Außerdem werden wir die wichtigsten Zahlen betrachten.

5   Wie ich bereits erwähnte, gebe ich Ihnen zunächst einen kurzen Überblick.

6   Laut dieser Studie sind unsere Kunden damit zufrieden.

14 **It's your turn now. Prepare the main part of a presentation using phrases from this unit.**
Use the checklist to help.

CHECKLIST FOR THE MAIN PART OF A PRESENTATION

☑ 1   Briefly state your topic again.

☑ 2   State your objective(s).

☑ 3   Signal the beginning of each part.

☑ 4   Talk about your topic.

☑ 5   Signal the end of each part.

☑ 6   Highlight the main points.

☑ 7   Summarize the main ideas.

☑ 8   Signal the end of the main part.

Infomedia, a German telecommunications company, gives some tips on what their employees should remember when presenting to English-speaking audiences. Read this text from their company newsletter and discuss the questions which follow.

Aled's Presentation Tips

As you all know, INFOMEDIA has been able to establish some important new business contacts with partners in the US this year. This also means that the need for English in meetings and presentations has increased. That's why we have asked our American colleague Aled Hughes from our Miami office to share a few tips with us.

Clear and simple structure

Remember that your audience will benefit most from a very clear and logical structure. Don't overload the audience and try to use simple language.

Your introduction

Some experts say this is the most important part of your presentation. In the first few minutes you can get your audience's attention, build rapport and create a positive impression.

Topic and objective

Clearly say what the topic and objective (or purpose) of your talk is. Repeat the topic and objective at some later time.

Signposting

Let the audience know at all times what you want to do and how you want to do it. This method is common in the American business world – so use it!

Repeating new information

Always repeat new details. This helps your audience to remember them and ensures optimal flow of information.

Summarizing points

At the end of each section summarize the main facts to make sure everybody is following.

Interaction with the audience

American audiences expect direct interaction. So treat them as individuals; show them that you care about their individual needs.

Presenter's role

The presenter is often considered as important as his or her topic, and the presenter's role is to make sure the presentation – even one on a dry topic – is interesting and entertaining. To achieve this goal American presenters often use their personalities more and tend to be more enthusiastic than their German counterparts.

Over to you

Which of these tips do you find most useful? Can you add any other tips?
Have you ever presented to an American audience? Did you think it was in any way different from a German audience?

My next slide shows …

Do you know the English names of these media and tools used in presentations?

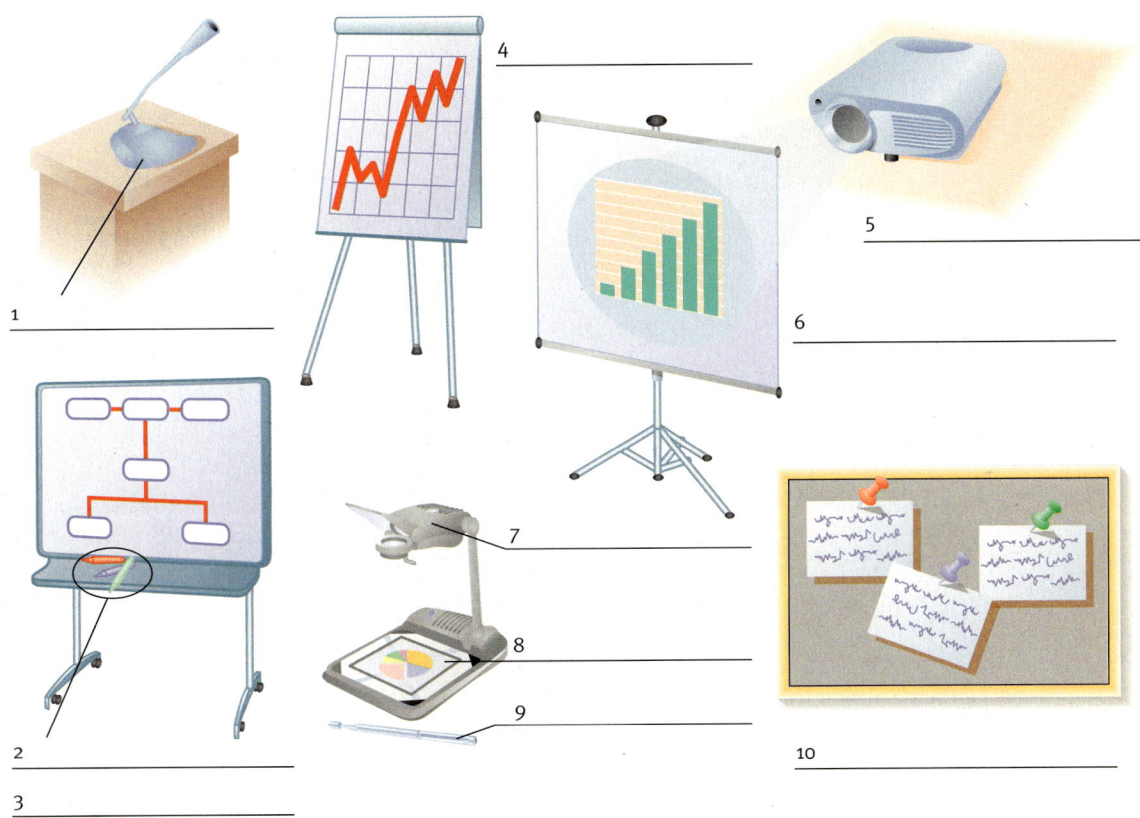

1 _____

2 _____

3 _____

4 _____

5 _____

6 _____

7 _____

8 _____

9 _____

10 _____

When, if ever, do you use the above media and tools in presentations? Which do you find the most effective? Why?

1 **Listen to the three extracts from presentations and tick [✓] the media used.**

16–18

	1	2	3
flip chart			
whiteboard			
PowerPoint slide			

16–18

2 **Now listen to the presentations again and complete the sentences.**

Presentation 1

1 Take a look at _____ .

2 They clearly _____ how a combination of two significant external factors affected our business in the first _____ of this year.

3 I'll just write some _____ on the _____ and then we will go on to discuss the next point.

Presentation 2

4 OK. Let's now _____ at our new magnetic ski rack Matterhorn which was launched in August.

5 On the _____ you will see an _____ of the Matterhorn X-15.

Presentation 3

6 These are the _____ for Germany for the _____ three quarters of this year.

7 As you _____ here, we've had a very successful year.

8 To highlight our success even further, let's _____ to the 2003 figures on the previous _____ .

9 Let me just _____ to it.

3 **Match parts from each column to make sentences used to refer to media.**

1 On the next page
2 My next slide shows
3 As you can see
4 Let me just show you some
5 To illustrate this
6 Let's now have a closer look
7 Here we can see how many
8 I have a slide

a from this picture, the design is absolutely new.
b customers have complained about the service.
c how much the market has changed.
d I'll show you our latest poster.
e at the figures on the next page.
f which shows the market development in 2005.
g interesting details.
h you will see a photo of the new XTK model.

SAYING NUMBERS

Numbers, especially long ones, are often difficult for the audience to understand. Try to say numbers slowly and clearly, and point at them while speaking.

2m	two million	235m²	two hundred and thirty-five square metres
1.6bn	one point six billion	98%	ninety-eight per cent
1/3, 3/4	one-third, three-quarters	€150,000	one hundred and fifty thousand euro(s)

Remember that ...
1 we use a comma in English to show thousands and a point to show the decimal place.
2 a 'billion' in English-speaking countries means *Milliarde* in German.
3 we say '2 million' or '10 billion' (not ~~2 millions/10 billions~~).
4 we say '2 million dollar**s**', '170 pound**s**' (not ~~2 million dollar/170 pound~~), but 'euro' can be either singular or plural.

19

4 How do you say these numbers in English? Write the number out in full, then listen to check your answers.

1 251 _____

_____

2 7,489 _____

_____

3 3.8 bn _____

4 € 49 m _____

5 $19.62 _____

6 2/3 _____

7 175 m² _____

8 1,240,000 _____

_____

9 7.2 _____

20–22

5 Listen to the three presentations and fill in the missing numbers below.

1

Car sales in 2004, 1st & 2nd quarter

	1st quarter	2nd quarter
Germany	_____1	19,600
EU	32,000	_____2
Non-EU	_____3	17,300

2

New open-plan office in Hamburg

- dimensions: _____4 x 16 m
- area: _____5
- 12th floor
- move on 15 February

3

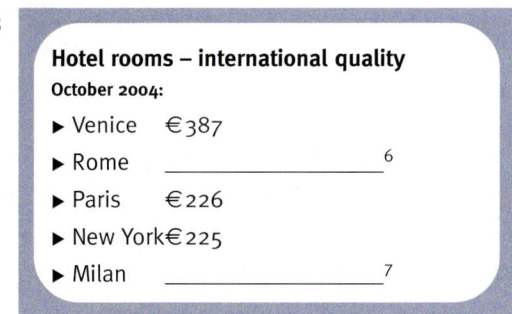

Hotel rooms – international quality
October 2004:
▶ Venice €387
▶ Rome _____6
▶ Paris €226
▶ New York €225
▶ Milan _____7

VOCABULARY ASSISTANT

average *durchschnittlich*
open-plan office *Großraumbüro*
premises *Geschäftsräume*

6 **It is often better to use approximate numbers in presentations as they are easier for the audience to understand and remember. Put the following words in the correct column in the table.**

> a little less than • about • almost • approximately • around •
> just over • just under • nearly • roughly • well over

– (less)	+/– (about the same)	+ (more)

Rewrite the sentences replacing the exact numbers with approximate ones using words from the table. Give at least two alternatives for each.

1 Last year we sold 90,083 mobile phones in Italy.

  Last year we sold a little more than / just over 90,000 mobile phones in Italy.

2 14.8% of the people asked said they were unhappy with the new design.

3 We will be spending €1.98 m on this technology.

4 Our laboratory says the ideal temperature is 18.1°C.

5 It will cost $3.97 to produce this item.

6 The new office is 389 m².

7 **Look at this short excerpt from a presentation and the two examples of PowerPoint slides on the next page. Which slide is more effective? Why?**

> *Let's look at the biggest car manufacturer in China, SAIC.
> The next slide shows some figures for 2003.
> SAIC manages a network of 55 subsidiaries and 63 joint
> ventures for cars and parts. The group employs more than
> 60,000 people and produced 800,000 vehicles in 2003,
> generating sales of about $12 billion.*

1

> **SAIC Group 2003**
>
> ⟳ subsidiaries: 55
> ⟳ joint ventures: 63
> ⟳ employees: 60,000
> ⟳ vehicles: 800,000
> ⟳ sales: $12 bn

2

> **2003 – Car Production of SAIC in China**
>
> • has 55 subsidiaries and 63 joint ventures
> • employs more than 60,000 people
> • produces about 800,000 vehicles
> • generates sales of $12 billion

THE RULE OF SIX

When presenting text on overheads or PowerPoint slides, it is a good idea to use the 'rule of six' which means:
• a maximum of six lines per slide
• a maximum of six words per line
If you stick to this rule, you won't risk overloading your bullet charts with too much information.

---

8   **Listen to the two short excerpts from presentations. Complete the slides and find headlines.**

23–24

1

> _____
> • more _____
>   – customers can change colours
>   – _____ colours to choose
>   from
> • circular shelving _____
> • _____ design

2

> _____
> • _____% 'wait and see'
> • _____% never
> • _____% yes, immediately

Now listen again and complete the sentences below.

1   Let's now _____ , which is ...

2   _____ to three new design features.

3   _____ is that customers can change the colour

    panels ...

4   What _____ ? Well, I think you'll agree that the

    results are _____ .

5   _____ nearly

    35 per cent said ...

6   _____ ?

    Well, let me tell you ...

> **VOCABULARY ASSISTANT**
> circular *Rund-*
> conventional *herkömmlich*
> floor space *Nutzfläche*

EMPHASIZING IMPORTANT POINTS

Using a verb ('stress', 'emphasize', etc)
I'd like to **stress** the following point.
I'd like to **draw your attention** to the latest figures.
I'd like to **emphasize** that our market position is excellent.

Using 'what'
What is really important is how much we are prepared to invest.
What we should do is talk about intercultural problems.

Rhetorical questions
So, just how good are the results?
So, where do we go from here?
Why do I say that? Because …

Adverb + adjective construction
It would be **completely wrong** to change our strategy at this point.
We compared the two offers and found the first one **totally unacceptable**.
I think this fact is **extremely important**.

---

9 **Make sentences using parts from each column.**

1 What I'd like to do	a important advertising is for us.
2 I'd like to highlight the	b for our success?
3 So, what are the reasons	c this model is selling quite well in the US.
4 I'd like to point out how	d turnover last year was excellent.
5 It's interesting to note that	e is discuss the latest sales figures.
6 I should repeat that our	f is the quality of these programs?
7 What we can't do is	g main problem areas.
8 So, just how good	h increase our budget.

10 **Complete the sentences with the correct adverb-adjective construction from the list.**

extremely dangerous • absolutely safe • incredibly cheap • highly interesting •
absolutely necessary • surprisingly good • completely useless

1 What we should remember is that this chemical process is _____ .

2 It's _____ to improve the quality of our products if we want
to win new customers.

3 This is a _____ point.

4 You will be pleased to hear that our turnover last month was _____
_____ .

5 Unfortunately, we found that some of the test results are _____
_____ .

6 I'm pleased to say that the crash test shows that this system is _____
_____ .

7 Right now this item only costs $1.50 – I think that's _____ .

11 **First complete this excerpt from a presentation with words from the box. Then listen and check.**

> let's talk about • draw your attention • have a look • it's quite remarkable •
> on the other hand • the figures also show that • you'll see that • can we explain

I'd now like to _____[1] to the regions where poverty has been reduced. If you look at the bar chart on the left, _____[2] that the proportion of global population living on less than $1 a day has dropped. _____ _____[3] in South Asia the proportion of extremely poor people has been reduced from 41 to 31%. _____ _____[4] how much progress has been made by China. _____[5], poverty has increased in many parts of Africa, Latin America and Eastern Europe. How _____[6] this uneven development? To answer this question, we'll _____[7] at the latest study from the World Bank. First, _____[8] the figures that indicate global progress.

12 **Are these words and expressions used to make contrasts or describe results? Put them into the correct category.**

Making contrasts	Describing results
_____	_____
_____	_____
_____	_____
_____	_____
_____	_____

on the other hand   thus   although

consequently   however   therefore

whereas   as a result

while   nevertheless   despite

Now complete the sentences with the correct alternative.

1 Online banking is mainly used by our younger customers. Many of our older customers consequently/however/therefore find it difficult to handle modern computer technology.

2 However/Whereas/Although the euro is quite strong, we managed to increase our exports to the US.

3 Whereas/Therefore/Despite we made a profit of $240,000 last year, this year's profit is only $110,000.

4 On the other hand/Despite/Although the growing demand, we didn't sell more cars than the year before.

5 We have to pay more for oil and gas. Consequently/However/Despite our products have become more expensive.

6 Poster campaigns are extremely important. Thus/On the other hand/As a result we also need advertisements in daily newspapers.

13 Translate these sentences. Try to use expressions from this unit.

1 Lassen Sie uns jetzt diese Tabelle näher betrachten.

2 Auf der nächsten Folie sehen Sie die Verkaufszahlen für das erste Quartal.

3 Wir verkaufen fast 30% unserer Produkte an andere europäische Länder.

4 Ich würde gern Ihre Aufmerksamkeit auf folgende Fakten lenken.

5 Trotz der Softwareprobleme konnten wir ein überraschend gutes Ergebnis erzielen.

6 Ich möchte gern betonen wie wichtig diese Änderung ist.

14 It's your turn now. Prepare bullet charts based on your own data (or take information from the first three of the following 'Summing up' texts on the next page). Find an effective headline for each bullet chart and present them to a partner.

CHECKLIST FOR VISUALS

☑ 1 Prepare each visual carefully and separately.
☑ 2 Check whether the visual really shows what you are saying.
☑ 3 Make sure your audience can read the visual (font size and colours).
☑ 4 Find effective headlines.
☑ 5 Keep design and content simple.
☑ 6 Use bullet charts for text.
☑ 7 Reduce text to a minimum.
☑ 8 Always prepare audience for visuals.
☑ 9 Present information clearly and logically.
☑ 10 Remember the rule of six.

What is important when presenting visuals? Which opinion(s) do you agree with?

Karen Hamilton, Marketing Manager

I think to be effective a good visual must focus on only a few points. It's important not to have too much information on one slide or transparency. Slide overload is bad because people will then spend time reading the slide rather than listening to the presenter. I normally use bullet points to structure information – I never write complete sentences. Headlines are important too.

Keith Sallis, Real Estate Manager

In my opinion the presenter is the focus of the presentation – not the visuals. The key purpose for using a visual aid is to help the audience understand the topic better. So the visuals should only be used to support the presenter's message. A process-flowchart slide, for example, helps people understand visually what you are describing verbally. If a visual distracts the audience's attention from what you're saying, it's useless.

Susan Liu, Export Manager

Above all, a slide or an overhead must be readable. If the audience can't read the slide, they will soon give up. That's why font size is very important. It should be as large as possible, I'd say at least 24. And sometimes it's also a good idea to use different colours to highlight some points. Using many different colours can be confusing though.

Bärbel Jäger, Market Researcher

What you say and what you show should always go together 100%. So when you're not talking about the slide, it shouldn't be visible. I always switch off the display when I'm talking about something that has nothing to do with the slide. If people are busy looking at the slide, they aren't listening to what you're saying. It's better to use the B-key to return to a black screen or replace the slide with some form of 'wallpaper' such as a company logo.

Jürgen Bogner, Financial Analyst

For me it's very important that the presenter *speaks* to the audience and doesn't *read* to them! The speaker must make eye-contact and not watch the monitor or screen while he or she is talking. I think it's extremely boring when someone just reads slides word for word as if it were an essay or something.

Tony Benetti, Media Consultant

It's called 'Death by PowerPoint' when people use so many sound effects and animations that the audience's attention is completely taken away from the delivery of the message. I think PowerPoint is a fantastic tool, but just because it has so many effects you don't have to use them all. Overuse is overkill here.

Over to you

What kinds of tools and visuals do you normally use in your presentations?
What tips can you think of for using visuals effectively?

As you can see from this graph ...

What are these visuals called in English? Match the numbers to the descriptions.

bar chart ☐   flow chart ☐   pie chart ☐
table ☐   map ☐   organizational chart / organigram ☐
technical drawing ☐   diagram ☐   (line) graph ☐

1

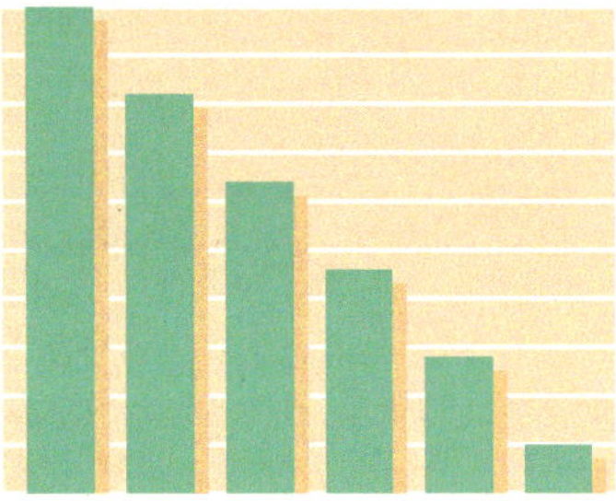

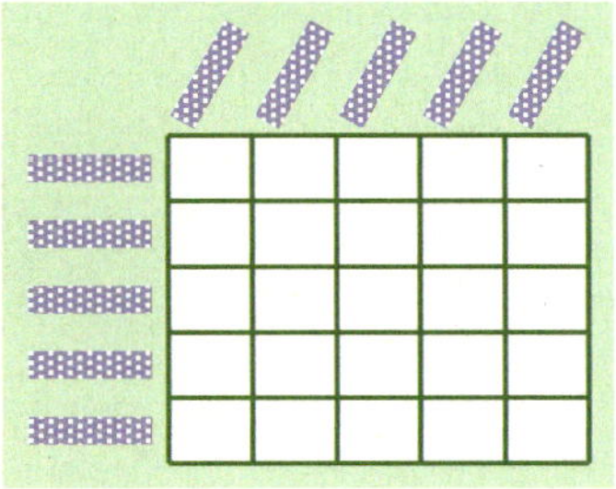

4

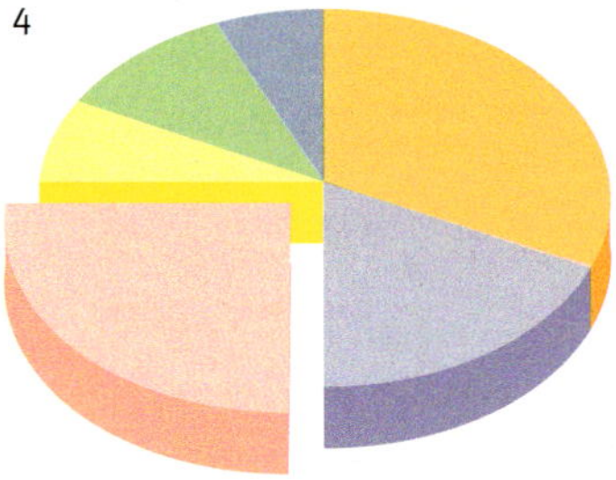

7

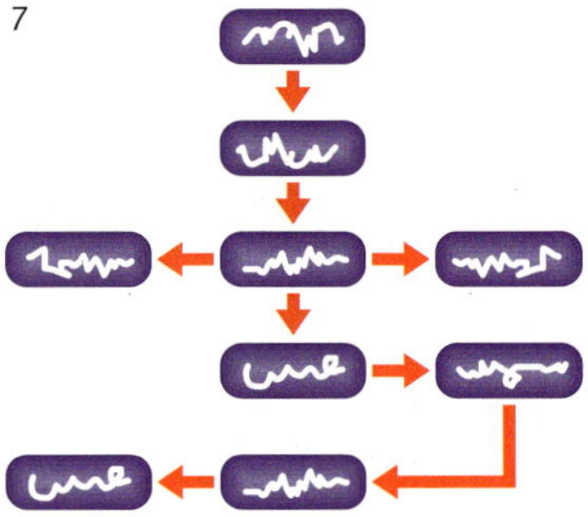

2

5

8

3

6

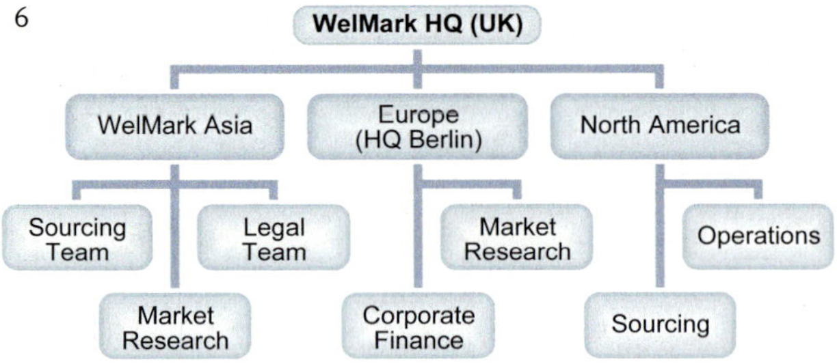

WelMark HQ (UK)

WelMark Asia — Europe (HQ Berlin) — North America

Sourcing Team   Legal Team   Market Research   Operations

Market Research   Corporate Finance   Sourcing

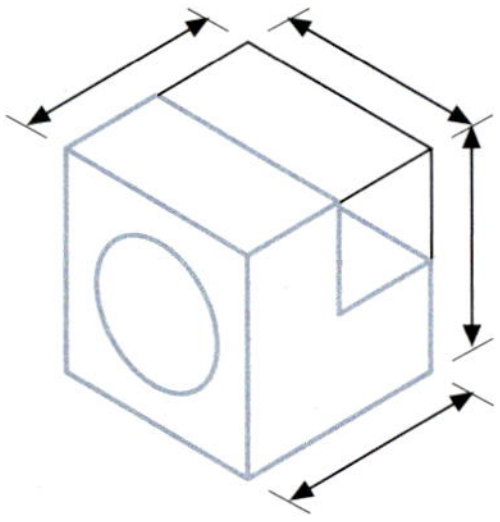

Which of these visuals would you use to describe ...

a your company's market share?
b the steps to be followed from order placement to delivery of a product?
c your company's new organizational structure?

1   **Listen to excerpts from three presentations and say what visuals are used.**

26–28

Presentation 1: _____   Presentation 2: _____   Presentation 3: _____

Now listen again and complete the sentences.

Presentation 1

1   The next _____ shows the _____ by age in our company.

2   You can see that the biggest _____ (...) indicates the _____ of employees in the age group 30 to 50.

Presentation 2

3   Let's now _____ at the sales figures over the past five years.

4   The key in the bottom _____ corner shows you which colour _____ which area.

5   OK, so I'd like to first _____ your attention to the sales figures for France – that's the blue line here.

Presentation 3

6   Now I'd like you to _____ at this next _____ which shows how the cost of living developed in Germany between 2000 and 2004.

7   If you look at the _____ on the _____, you will see that the highest increase was in 2001 with a rise of 2 _____.

TALKING ABOUT VISUALS

The first rule of preparing effective visuals is that they should be clear and easy for the audience to follow. However, sometimes it is necessary to explain a more complicated visual and it is always necessary to point out the most important information.

Explaining a visual
Let's now look at the next slide which shows ...
First, let me quickly explain the graph.
You can see that different colours have been used to indicate ...
The key in the bottom left-hand corner shows you ...

Highlighting information
I'd like to start by drawing your attention to ...
What I'd like to point out here is ...
I think you'll be surprised to see ...
I'd like you to focus your attention on ...
Let's look more closely at ...

---

2   **Which is the box ...**

1   in the centre? ☐
2   in the bottom left-hand corner? ☐
3   across the top? ☐
4   down the left side of the slide? ☐
5   on the left? ☐
6   in the upper right-hand corner? ☐
7   across the bottom? ☐
8   on the right? ☐

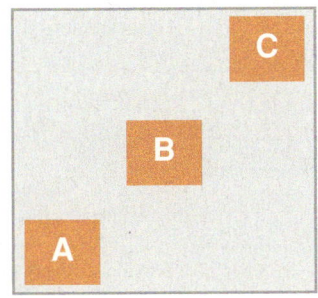
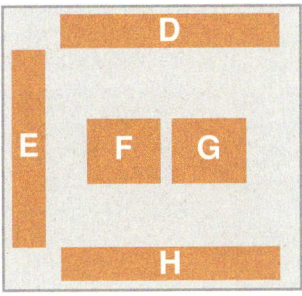

3   **Match 1–10 with a–j to make sentences used to talk about visuals.**

1   Let's now have a look
2   The black line gives us
3   Each line on the graph indicates
4   In the upper right-hand corner
5   The graph on the following slide
6   Now I'd like you to take
7   The names of the new models are listed
8   You can see the test results in the
9   This aspect of the problem is illustrated in
10 I'd like to draw your

a   shows our revenues sinces 2004.
b   the next pie chart.
c   at how the new division will be structured.
d   attention to the figures in the left-hand column.
e   you can see the specifications for the TP model.
f   the sales figures for the VW Fox.
g   table on the right.
h   a look at the next slide.
i   the production output of a different product.
j   across the top.

4   **A head of department from a private medical insurance company is telling colleagues from the Italian parent company about last year's health spending. Look at how she describes this pie chart and complete the gaps with words from the list.**

account • amount • attention • divided • see • shown • surprised • total

This pie chart shows our total health spending for the last year and how it is _____ [1] among the various health sector areas. Let's begin with the biggest area which is

_____ [2] in green. We can _____ [3] that 31% of our total health spending went into hospital care last year. The second biggest area with a _____ [4] of 23% is 'other spending' – that's the red segment here. It includes dental services and home health care. I think you'll be _____ [5] to see that nearly the same _____ [6] – that's 22% – was spent on doctors and clinical services. This was mainly because of the increase in medical technology costs. I'd now like to draw your _____ [7] to the prescription drugs which _____ [8] for 10% of our total costs.

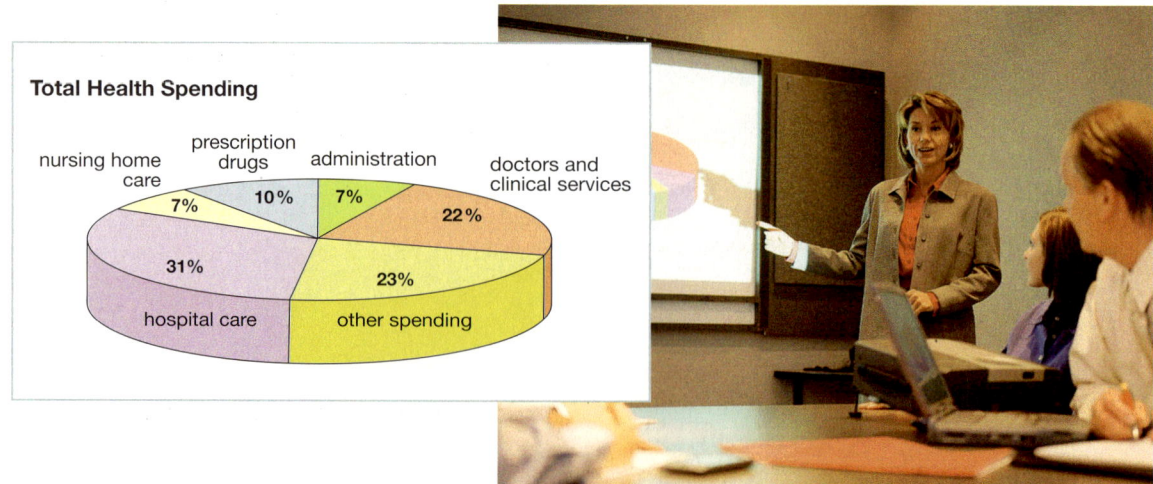

5 **Two presenters are describing graphs. Listen and complete the graphs.**

29–30

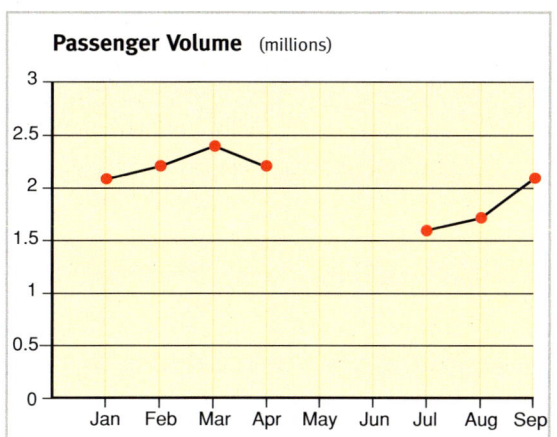

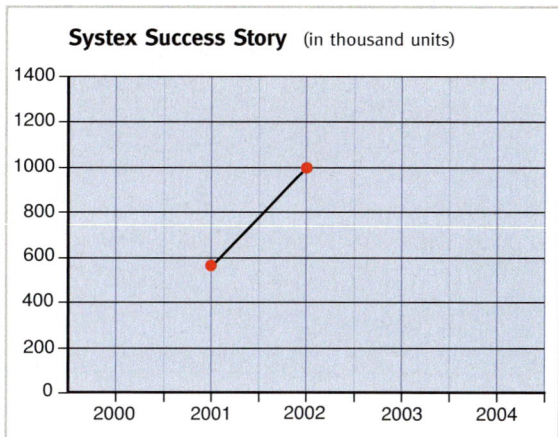

VOCABULARY ASSISTANT	to boost *ankurbeln*
	hay fever *Heuschnupfen*
	to pick up *zunehmen*
	to rocket *in die Höhe schnellen*
	to slump *sinken, stürzen*

6 **Complete these sentences from the two excerpts with words from the lists. Then listen again to check.**

29

Presentation 1

> decline • fall • fluctuated • picking up • reached • rose • slumped

1 As you can see here, passenger numbers _____ between 2.1 and 2.3 million in the first four months.

2 They even _____ moderately in May ...

3 In June you'll notice a sharp _____ in passenger numbers ...

4 Passenger traffic _____ to about 1.5 million – a _____ of almost 40%.

5 As a result, ticket sales started _____ in July.

6 By the end of September passenger numbers had _____ just over 2 million.

30

Presentation 2

> increase • rocketed • rose • stood • went down

1 The figure _____ by about 50,000 in the following year.

2 In 2002, however, sales _____ to 1 million ...

3 2003 even saw a further _____ in sales to 1.3 million ...

4 As expected, sales _____ again in 2004 and _____ at just over a million at the end of the year.

7 These verbs are used to describe movement or trends. Put them in the correct category: upward, downward or other form of movement.

climb • decline • decrease • double • drop • expand • fall • fluctuate •
go down • go up • grow • hit a low • increase • pick up • plunge • reach a high •
recover • remain stable • rise • stabilize • stay the same

Upward ↗

_____
_____
_____
_____
_____
_____
_____
_____
_____

Downward ↘

_____
_____
_____
_____
_____
_____
_____

Other

_____
_____
_____
_____

TALKING ABOUT TRENDS (SIMPLE PAST AND PRESENT PERFECT)

We use the simple past to talk about a movement or trend which happened in the past and is now finished. Signal words for the simple past are 'last month/year', 'in January', 'from 1997–2001', 'during the oil crisis', etc.

In April the rate of unemployment **rose** to 5 million.
Between May and July our export business almost **doubled**.
In 2003 alone China's car production **increased** by 85%.

We use the present perfect to talk about a movement or trend which started in the past but is not yet finished. Signal words are 'since' (since August), 'for' (for five years), 'this month/year' or expressions with 'over' (over the past six months).

The number of German investors **has declined** since 1998. *(It is still declining …)*
The US economy **has grown** rapidly over the past four months. *(It is still growing …)*

Note the difference between 'rise' and 'raise'.

to rise *(auf)steigen*	**to raise sth** *etw erhöhen*
Petrol prices **rose** again in May.	The oil industry **raised** prices last year.
The number of tourists **has risen** to 2.6 million.	The European Central Bank **has raised** interest rates.

8   **Use the notes to make sentences in the simple past or present perfect.**

1   telephone costs/rise/since January

   Telephone costs have risen since January.

2   sales/drop/at the beginning of the year

   _____

3   energy consumption/increase/over the past 30 years

   _____

4   gas prices/go up/last month

   _____

5   number of customers/grow/since 2004

   _____

6   surprisingly/interest rates/fall/yesterday

   _____

7   TBN's share price/hit a low/after the crash in 1999

   _____

8   online bookings/double/since May last year

   _____

9   between May and July/order volume/fluctuate

   _____

Rewrite sentences 1–6 to express the opposite.

1   *Telephone costs have fallen since January.* _____

2   _____

3   _____

4   _____

5   _____

6   _____

9   **Read the following sentences and check whether 'rise' and 'raise' have been used correctly. If not, correct the sentence.**

1   We haven't raised prices since 1 January 2003.
2   Unemployment raised to a record high at the beginning of this year.
3   Why did they rise their rates last December?
4   Train fares in Germany have risen by 5% in the past two years.
5   Interest rates will raise again this year.
6   The company rose the dividends in March.

10   **Choose the correct verbs to complete the sentences.**

1   Productivity has hit a low/has gone down/fell in November.

2   Output climbed up/has improved/recovered since 2003.

3   After the takeover in May sales grew up/have decreased/plunged.

4   This year our market share raised/has grown/dropped down by 10%.

5   Staff numbers have doubled/rose up/have raised this year.

6   In 2004 sales have climbed/slumped/have risen.

11   **The sentences below can be used to describe the graph on the right. Put them in the correct order. Then listen to check.**

31

- [ ]   a   In June, however, the programme's market share plunged to 6%.

- [ ]   b   Over the next three months, the figures continued to rise steadily and reached record levels each month: 11% in July, 12% in August and 14% in September.

- [ ]   c   The next graph shows the market share of *Lifestyle Today* for the first six months after it was launched in April 2005.

- [ ]   d   This drastic decline has a simple cause. We lost a large part of our audience to live transmissions of two major sporting events: Wimbledon and the Confederations Cup.

- [ ]   e   As you can see, we started off with a rather low market share of about 7%.

- [ ]   f   Fortunately, this was only a temporary setback.

- [ ]   g   Audience ratings improved significantly, climbing to 10% in May.

Lifestyle Today

Match words from column A and B to make word partnerships from the text.

A	B
drastic	significantly
improve	setback
rise	steadily
temporary	decline

VOCABULARY ASSISTANT

launch   *Einführung*
rating   *Quote*
setback   *Rückschlag*

TALKING ABOUT TRENDS (ADJECTIVES AND ADVERBS)

Adjectives + nouns	Adverbs + verbs
There was a **sudden** <u>increase</u> in prices.	Sales <u>increased</u> **slightly** in summer.
In August, we notice a **moderate** <u>fall</u>.	Over the past two years the number <u>has dropped</u> **significantly**.
This was followed by a **gradual** <u>decline</u>.	Last month the rates <u>rose</u> **sharply**.

---

12 **Complete the sentences with the correct form of the verb/adverb combinations in the box. The symbols indicates what kind of movement is described.**

> decline slightly • decrease steadily • fall dramatically •
> grow considerably • ~~increase slightly~~ • rise sharply

1   The line graph shows that turnover _has increased slightly_____ since May. ➚

2   You can see here that interest rates _____ at the beginning

   of 2004. ↓

3   Over the past six months, sales _____. ➘

4   The oil price _____ after the fire in an oilfield. ↑

5   The number of online stores _____ this year. ➚

6   Our sales force _____ since 2001. ↘

---

13 **Rewrite the sentences using an adjective + noun expression and one of the sentence beginnings below.**

> There was/has been ... • This was followed by ... • We have seen ...

1   Turnover has increased slightly since May.

   _There has been a slight increase in turnover since May._____

2   Income fell sharply last year.

   _This was followed by a_____

3   The number of jobs has declined drastically this year.

   _____

4   Hotel rates dropped slightly in Munich.

   _____

5   Tourist numbers increased suddenly.

   _____

6   Social security costs have grown steadily.

   _____

14   **Sometimes it is necessary to interpret the visual, for example by explaining the reason behind a fact (the cause) or its consequence (the effect). Use words from each column to make sentences.**

1 There are several	caused	for the decrease in productivity.
2 We chose this method	has led	a new overtime policy.
3 The	resulted	by the collapse of one of our partner firms.
4 Our new policy	reasons	of this move was a drastic increase in our costs.
5 The slump was	thanks to	to a significant rise in sales.
6 Downsizing	and	in a drastic fall in staff numbers.
7 We increased our prices	because	our sales went up!
8 Our output has doubled	result	we needed reliable figures.

Which sentences above explain …

cause? _____

effect? _____

15   **Complete the sentences with the correct prepositions from the box.**

> around • at • between • by • from • in • of • to • until

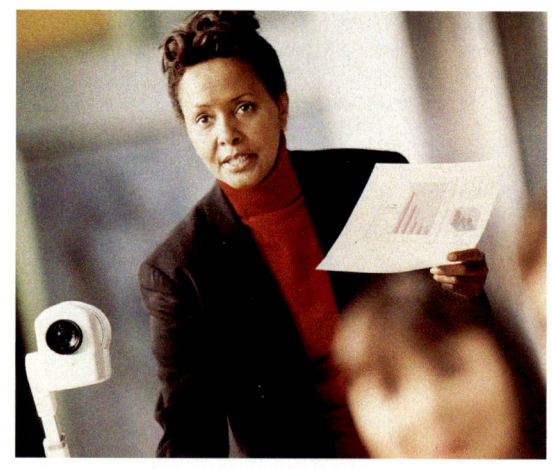

"The graph shows our online sales figures for the EU market _____[1] 2004. In the first quarter, online sales averaged _____[2] 50,000 and 52,000 euros. In April, sales increased _____[3] 61,000 euros and remained steady _____[4] the end of the second quarter. In the third quarter we notice a sharp rise _____[5] 61,000 to 87,000 euros, an increase _____[6] almost 50 per cent. In October and November, sales fluctuated _____[7] the 85,000 euro mark. This was followed by a slight decline in December, with online sales falling _____[8] 10 per cent, reaching 73,000 euros _____[9] the end of the year."

16   **Translate these sentences. Try to use expressions from this unit.**

1 Dieses Tortendiagramm zeigt unseren Marktanteil in Prozent.
2 Laut der Studie sind die Reisekosten seit 2000 stark gestiegen.
3 Die Zinsen wurden Anfang des Jahres um 0,5 % erhöht.
4 Im Juni gab es einen drastischen Anstieg der Transportkosten um 15 %.
5 Unsere Produktivität erreichte im Dezember einen Tiefpunkt.
6 Der Grund für den Rückgang ist die schlechte Wirtschaftslage.

17   It's your turn now. Either describe one of the graphs in this unit or describe a graph or chart of your own. Try to use words and phrases from this unit to present the visual.

> ### CHECKLIST FOR USING VISUALS (GRAPHS & CHARTS)
>
> ☑ 1   Make your visual as clear and easy to understand as possible.
> ☑ 2   Start by telling your audience what the graph/chart illustrates.
> ☑ 3   Highlight the key points.
> ☑ 4   Say why these points are important (and explain the cause or effect).
> ☑ 5   Use different verbs to express movement/development.
> ☑ 6   Use the same key words and phrases you used on your bullet charts.

What advice would you give someone who has to describe trends on graphs and charts? Work with a partner to make a list of tips. Then read what advice 'James & Gillham', an international firm providing financial services, give on their intranet.

J&G   James & Gillham

Presenting trends and financial developments is our daily business. Here are some guidelines you should follow when you next use a graph or chart in your presentation.

1   Think about the number of visuals you want to use – don't overdo it! Remember: less is often more!

2   Before showing the graph or chart, prepare the audience for it. Say something which makes them interested in what they will see. This technique is called 'media teasing'.

3   Give the audience time to understand what they see before you start explaining the details.

4   If the movement you want to describe is very complex, simplify it. Divide the graph into two or three parts and summarize the main developments.

5   Provide an interpretation of the graph's movement. The audience wants to know why there are ups and downs in the graph, what they mean and what consequences they have.

6   Use the TTT method when presenting graphics: **touch** (or point to) a detail on the projection, then **turn** to the audience, and finally, **talk** to them.

7   Use interesting and varied language to describe trends. You need alternative expressions to describe similar developments.

Over to you

Which of the tips above were on your list? Which are new?
Which of the tips do you think are the most useful?
How often do you have to describe charts or graphs in English? Which types of visuals do you use most frequently in your presentations?

To sum up …

Look at these final statements from different conclusions. Which ones do you find most effective? Work with a partner to rank them (1 = most effective, 8 = least effective).

a Thank you very much for your attention.

b In conclusion, I'd like to highlight our company's highly innovative products.

c So, to put it in the words of the famous H. Gordon Selfridge, "The customer is always right".

d Well, I don't know whether this was helpful but I'd like to leave it here.

e We have all the facts. Let's get to work now!

f The one last thing I'd like to say is: it's your choice.

g So, that's all I have to say. I hope you haven't all fallen asleep!

h To conclude, I want to come back to that story I told you at the start of my presentation and say one word: apple pie!

What do the presenters try to achieve with the different endings?

1 Listen to the conclusion of a presentation and answer the questions.

1 What was the brief?

2 What are the options?

3 What is the best solution?

4 What does the presenter recommend?

2 **Look at these sentences from the presentation and put them in the correct category in the box.**

1 I'll just run through the three different options ...
2 We'd suggest ...
3 Now I'll be happy to answer any questions you may have.
4 We'd therefore recommend that we ...
5 Before I stop, let me go through my main points again.
6 Well, this brings me to the end of my presentation.

CONCLUSION OF A PRESENTATION

Signalling the end of the presentation

_____
_____
_____
_____
_____

Summarizing the main points

_____
_____
_____
_____

Recommending or suggesting something

_____
_____
_____
_____

Inviting questions

_____
_____
_____
_____

Now add these phrases to the table above.

a Thank you all for listening.

b In my opinion, we should ...

c We just have time for a few questions.

d To sum up then, we ...

e OK, I think that's everything I wanted to say ...

g I'd like to run through my main points again ...

f Are there any questions?

h As a final point, I'd like to ...

i I'm now nearing the end of my talk ...

j Just to summarize the main points of my talk ...

k What I'd like to suggest is ...

3 Unscramble the sentences to make typical sentences from a conclusion.

1   Well,/the end of/today/brings me/to/my talk/that

_____

2   Before I/key issues/go over/the/stop,/let me/again

_____

3   As a/means/let me say/for us/what this/final point,

_____

4   Finally,/like to/issue/highlight/I'd/one/key

_____

5   To sum/looked at/product range/up then,/the new/first/we

_____

6   That/logistics/just about/to say/about/I wanted/everything/covers

_____

4 Complete the sentences with words from the box.

> come back • figures we have • final point • briefly summarize •
> my opinion • now approaching • suggest that • to highlight

1   If I may _____ the pros and cons.

2   Based on the _____ , it is clear
    that we must act quickly.

3   Well, I'm _____ the end of my
    talk.

4   OK, I'd now like _____ the key
    figures.

5   Let me make one _____ .

6   In _____ , we need a new sales
    strategy.

7   Let me _____ to the key issue.

8   I _____ we work together with our French partners.

5 Use the notes on the next page and follow the flow chart to practise the end of two talks.

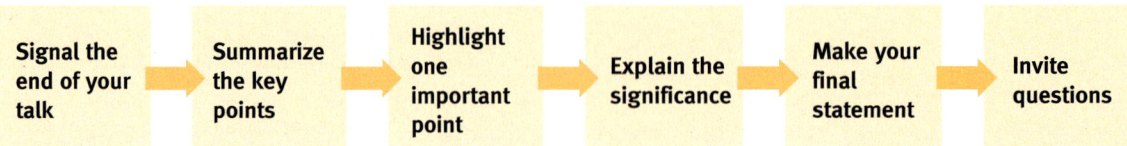

| Signal the end of your talk | → | Summarize the key points | → | Highlight one important point | → | Explain the significance | → | Make your final statement | → | Invite questions |

Update on new software project

Main points
- talked about delays with first trials & how we're dealing with them
- reviewed partners involved in project/how we can work with them most effectively*
- the next steps – where we go from here

(a lot of experience in this area, good reputation for quality)

* Key point: IRG Design is involved!! Important to success of project!

6 **Listen to four conclusions and say which technique is used in which presentation (1–4).**

33–36

Technique	Presentation
Call to action	☐
Story	☐
Question	☐
Quotation	☐

> **VOCABULARY ASSISTANT**
> competitiveness *Wettbewerbsfähigkeit*
> to share *teilen, gemeinsam nutzen können*
> to strengthen *stärken*

Which sentences (a–d) come from which presentation? Write the number of the presentation in the box. Then listen again and complete the gaps.

☐ a So, _____ this opportunity to get ahead of our competitors?

☐ b I'd just like to _____ former US president Bill Clinton once said: "You can put wings on a pig, but you don't make it an eagle".

☐ c _____ . Set up an appointment with our project manager and our SAP consultant and we can work out the Best Practice solutions that suit your business.

☐ d _____ I told at the start of my talk. _____, the sales meeting in Vienna with the disappointed Japanese businessmen? … _____ _____ that knowing your entire product range is the key to success.

EFFECTIVE CONCLUSIONS

Using questions
After all, isn't that why we're here?
Let me just finish with a question: If we don't do it, won't somebody else?

Quoting a well-known person
As … once said, …
To quote a well-known businessman, …
To put it in the words of …, …

Referring back to the beginning
Remember what I said at the beginning of my talk today? Well, …
Let me just go back to the story I told you earlier. Remember, …

Calling the audience to action
So that's the plan. Now let's go and put it into practice!
So now it's your turn.
Now let's make a real effort to achieve this goal!

7 Match 1–7 with a–g to make final statements from conclusions.

1 To put it in the words of Albert Einstein,
2 I would like to finish my talk
3 Let me go back to
4 So, now it's
5 Remember that story I told you
6 As the famous basketball coach Pat Riley said:
7 OK, and now let's

a "Look for your choices, pick the best one, then go with it."
b with an important question.
c about the new branch in Tokyo?
d get down to work!
e what I said at the start of this talk.
f "The important thing is not to stop questioning."
g up to you.

8 Complete the sentences with prepositions from the box.

about • by • for • in • on • out • through • to

1 Based _____ what we know, we can optimize our procedures.

2 _____ my opinion, we should go ahead with the project.

3 OK, this brings me _____ the end of my talk.

4 What does this mean _____ our business?

5 Let me just go _____ the key issues again.

6 We found _____ that our sales force needs more support.

7 Well, that's all I wanted to say _____ strategic planning.

8 We saw that the delays were caused _____ technical problems.

9 Use the clues to complete the crossword puzzle.

ACROSS
4 "I would like to begin my presentation with a … from a great leader.
5 The English word for '*vorschlagen*'.
6 "I will now … some important points for discussion."
9 Another verb for 'summarize'.
10 "OK, that's … I wanted to tell you about new technologies".

DOWN
1 What's the preposition? "Let me run … the main points again."
2 "After weighing the pros and …, we think a merger would be the best option."
3 The most important points or the … issues.
7 Another word for 'target'– I'm sure we can reach this … .
8 "These results are excellent. They show that we are on the right … ."

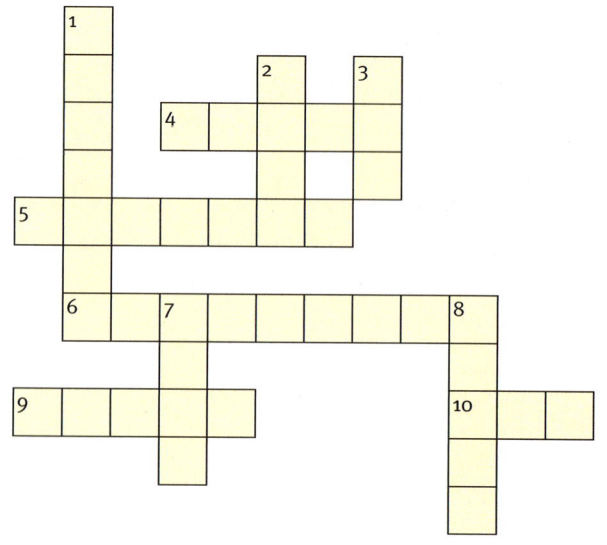

USING YOUR VOICE EFFECTIVELY

How you say something is often just as important as **what** you say. You can use your voice and the way you stress words or make pauses in sentences to make your presentation more interesting and easier for the audience to follow.

Stressing words

By emphasizing particular words or parts of words you create certain effects. Notice how you can change the meaning of a sentence by putting the stress on a different word.

We all know that this is an <u>extremely</u> difficult market. *(it's more than just difficult)*
We <u>all</u> know that this is an extremely difficult market. *(you and I agree on this)*
<u>We</u> all know that this is an extremely difficult market. *(but they don't)*

Making pauses

You can use pauses to slow your pace down and make your sentences easier to understand. Group words into phrases according to their meaning and make pauses between the phrases.

In my opinion we should go into other markets.
In my opinion // we should go // into other markets.

On the other hand, the figures prove that we are on the right track.
On the other hand, // the figures prove // that we are on the right track.

10 **Look at the clues in brackets and underline the word which should be stressed in each sentence.**

1 <u>Clearly,</u> we need to look at this again. *(it's obvious!)*
2 Clearly, we need to look at this <u>again</u>. *(twice wasn't enough)*

3 We will never get such a perfect opportunity again. *(this is our only chance)*
4 We will never get such a perfect opportunity again. *(but perhaps the competition will)*

5 I'd like us to work out a strategy. *(and nobody else)*
6 I'd like us to work out a strategy. *(a plan is important)*

7 There hasn't been a dramatic increase in production costs. *(but there has been an increase)*
8 There hasn't been a dramatic increase in production costs. *(the increase was in personnel costs)*

9 I think we've made a good start. *(but you might not agree)*
10 I think we've made a good start. *(but there is still a lot to do)*

Now work with a partner and practise reading out the sentence pairs with the correct stress. Can she or he hear the difference in meaning?

37

11 Read the following text. Underline the words which you think should be emphasized and use double slashes (//) for pauses in the sentences. Then listen and check.

> *Finally, let me come back to the key points of my talk.*
> *I told you that in the first quarter, more than half, or 52%,*
> *of eBay's revenues came from overseas. This is in line with the*
> *targets we set out in 2004 when we decided we wanted to*
> *continue to rely on overseas markets, especially China, to keep*
> *growing. In the past three months, we've added more new*
> *users in China than in any other country.*
> *Now what are our targets for the next few months? The first*
> *major step will be the introduction of our PayPal payment*
> *service in China. And then we will focus on finding customers*
> *in existing markets, such as the US and Germany, who haven't*
> *tried buying or selling on eBay yet.*

12 Translate the sentences. Try to use expressions from this unit.

1 Lassen Sie mich die wichtigsten Ergebnisse zusammenfassen.
2 Ich würde jetzt gerne noch einmal die Hauptpunkte durchgehen.
3 Meiner Meinung nach müssen wir unsere Verkaufsstrategie ändern.
4 Mein Vorschlag ist, dass wir uns auf den deutschen Markt konzentrieren.
5 Ich komme jetzt zum Ende meiner Präsentation.
6 Jetzt lassen sie uns das in die Tat umsetzen.

13 It's your turn now. Follow the checklist to practise making conclusions. Try to use words and phrases from the unit.

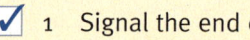

CHECKLIST FOR CONCLUSIONS

☑ 1 Signal the end of your talk.
☑ 2 Summarize the key points.
☑ 3 Highlight one important point.
☑ 4 Explain the significance.
☑ 5 Make your final statement.

On his website, the American presentations 'guru' Charlie F. Elroy, talks about his strategies for good conclusions.

Make a good *last* impression!

Don't forget that last impressions are just as important as first impressions. I personally think the end of your talk is even more important than the beginning because people tend to remember most the last thing that they are told.

Make them *listen*!

When you move from the main part to the conclusion, use a sentence that signals to the audience that now they really have to sit up and listen!

Make a *lasting* impression!

Your conclusion is the place to make sure that you have planted the key ideas of your talk in your listeners' minds. Don't miss this opportunity!

Charlie F. Elroy

Here are some of my strategies for effective conclusions:

1 **Summarizing the main points**
   This the most widely used method but borrrrrring!! However, sometimes you will find it's the best strategy. Just sum up the main points you have covered in the middle section.

2 **Quoting a famous person**
   Quote something from a famous person that fits the content of your talk and use it as a final statement. You can find lots of quotations on the Internet. If you can't find one, make it up. As long as it fits, no one will ever know.

Albert Einstein
Uncle Harry

3 **Asking a provocative question or making a surprising statement**
   Ask a question which surprises, shocks or provokes your audience – anything to make them think and to make a lasting impression. Or you can just say something unusual, unexpected or even shocking to help support your key points.

4 **Using the 'sandwich' technique**
   Think of your presentation as a sandwich with two slices of bread (introduction + conclusion) and the cheese in the middle (main part). The 'sandwich' strategy means that you have a connection between the beginning and the end of your talk. If, for example, you start telling a joke or (funny) story in the introduction, stop at an exciting moment and move on to the main part. Then finish the story/joke in the conclusion.

5 **Thanking the audience**
   Fugeddabowdit!* Forget standard phrases such as 'Thank you very much for your attention' or 'Thank you for listening'. After a good presentation, it is the audience who should be thanking you!

* forget about it!

Over to you

Which tips do you think are the most useful? Which are not useful at all? Why do you think that?
Can you think of any other strategies for making good conclusions?
How might cultural differences between you and the audience affect the way you end a presentation?
Do you remember a conclusion you found particularly effective? What did the presenter do?

6 Any other questions?

Work with a partner. Ask each other the questions below and make a note of the answers. Then tell the class what you found out.

1 Do you prefer questions during or after the presentation? Why?
2 How do you feel about the question period at the end of a presentation?
3 How do you prepare for the question period?
4 How do you deal with questions you don't want to answer?
5 What do you do if you can't answer the question?
6 How do you deal with dominant participants?
7 Do you remember a presentation in which questions were handled well/badly? What do you think went right/wrong?

1 **Listen to four excerpts from the question phase of a presentation. How does the presenter deal with the questions? Tick the correct box.**

38–41

	1	2	3	4
She answers the question.				
She doesn't answer.				
She doesn't know the answer.				
She doesn't understand the question.				

VOCABULARY ASSISTANT

application *Anwendung*
bug *Fehler (Software)*
trial run *Testlauf*

2 Listen again and complete the sentences from the presentation.

1 And now I'll be _____ any questions you may have. Yes?

2 You were talking about software problems. What exactly _____ by that?

3 Well, I _____ that the new software is being tested at the moment. (...)
   Does that answer your question?

4 _____ telling us whether the new software will help to improve our
   company's image?

5 I'm afraid I don't _____ your question. Could you be a bit more specific?

6 I have _____ . It's about the piloting stage. Which division will start piloting
   the software first?

7 If you _____ , I'd prefer not to discuss that today.

8 _____ , there will be a meeting next week where that will be decided. OK? ...

9 You spoke about special training courses earlier. _____ how they will be
   organized?

10 Sorry, _____ that's not my field. But I'm sure Linda Koll from the training
   department _____ that question.

DEALING WITH QUESTIONS

Asking for clarification
If you do not understand the question, politely ask the person to repeat or explain it.

> I'm sorry. Could you repeat your question, please?
> I'm afraid I didn't quite catch that.
> I'm afraid I don't quite understand your question.

Avoiding giving an answer
Sometimes you may not want to answer a question, perhaps because it's the wrong time for
it or the question is irrelevant. When avoiding giving an answer, make sure that your tone of
voice is friendly and your reply is polite.

> If you don't mind, I'd prefer not to discuss that today.
> Perhaps we could deal with this after the presentation / at some other time.
> I'm afraid that's not really what we're here to discuss today.

Admitting you don't know the answer
If you don't know the answer to a question, be honest and say so. Offer to find out or name
a person who can answer the question.

> Sorry, that's not my field. But I'm sure Peter Bott from Sales could answer your question.
> I'm afraid I don't know the answer to your question, but I'll try to find out for you.
> I'm afraid I'm not in a position to answer that. Perhaps Maria could help.

3   **Match 1–9 with a–i to make complete sentences.**

1   Good point, but I'd prefer   a   your question please?
2   Perhaps we could   b   deal with this at some other time.
3   Could you repeat   c   off the top of my head.
4   I'm afraid that's   d   not to discuss that today.
5   I'm sure Ms Maier   e   answer your question?
6   Sorry, I don't   f   not my field.
7   I'm afraid I don't know that   g   could answer that question for you.
8   I'm afraid I'm not   h   in a position to comment on that.
9   Does that   i   quite understand your question.

Now decide which of the sentences above you can use to ...

a   ask for clarification: _____

b   make it clear you don't want to answer the question: _____

c   admit you don't know the answer: _____

4   **Complete the dialogue with phrases from the box. Then listen and check.**

> Could you give us • Does that mean • Are there any questions •
> Go ahead • Excuse me • No, not at all • May I ask • I suggest you
> speak to • I'd be interested • Would you mind

Presenter   _____ [1]?

Susanne   Yes, I have a question. _____[2] some background information on Track
Ltd?

Presenter   Certainly. They're one of the leading manufacturers of outdoor equipment in the UK
with more than 35 factories worldwide.

Tim   _____[3] telling us why you've chosen them as partners?

Presenter   _____[4]. The answer's quite simple. We were very
impressed with the quality of their products and their prices are very attractive.

Annette   _____[5] a question?

Presenter   Yes, of course. _____[6].

Annette   _____[7] to know what their terms of payment are.

Presenter   I'm afraid I can't answer that question. _____[8] Sylvia Becker –
she would be the right person to ask.

Alex   _____[9]. You mentioned a German office. _____[10]
we do business through them?

Presenter   That's right. We need to discuss the details though.

ASKING POLITE QUESTIONS

There are different ways of asking questions in English. If you want to be more polite (and less aggressive), it is better to use less direct questions.

Direct questions
When do you plan to move to Geneva?
What is the project status?

Less direct questions
Could you tell me when you plan to move to Geneva?
Do you mind if I ask what the project status is?

Note that in polite questions it is often necessary to change the word order or add words like 'if' or 'whether'.
What's the current project status? ➔ Can you tell me **what** the current project status **is**?
Is that the final decision? ➔ Could you tell me **whether/if that's** the final decision?

---

5 **Look at the questions in the bubble and use the words given to make them more polite.**

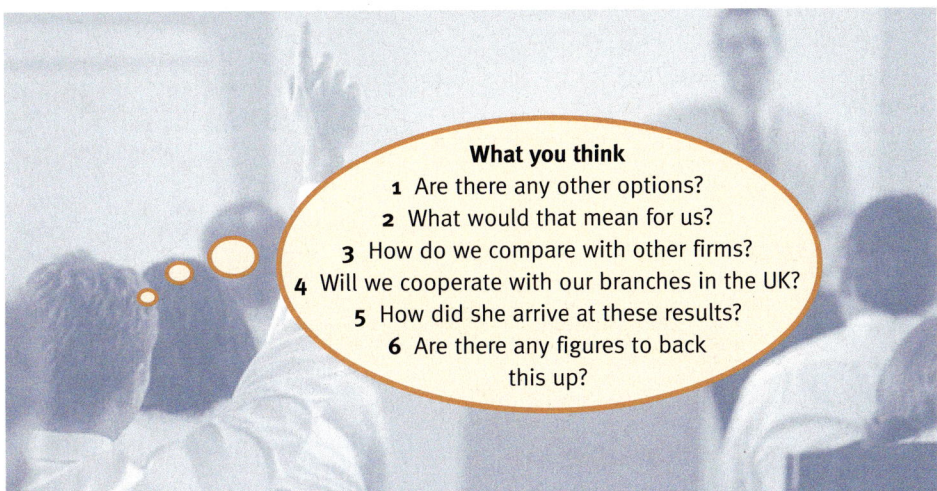

What you think
1 Are there any other options?
2 What would that mean for us?
3 How do we compare with other firms?
4 Will we cooperate with our branches in the UK?
5 How did she arrive at these results?
6 Are there any figures to back this up?

What you ask

1 May I ask *if there are any other options?*

2 Do you mind telling me *what that would mean for us?*

3 May I ask _____

4 Can you tell me _____

5 Would you mind telling me _____

6 Could you tell me _____

Now match the questions from above to the answers.

a Of course. Basically we have two alternatives. ...
b Well, first of all, more work for each of us.
c Yes, we will. I've already contacted the London office.
d Yes. As I said earlier, I'll be passing out handouts with the latest data.
e Very well. At the moment we are market leader.
f Not at all. They are based on the latest study.

ANTICIPATING QUESTIONS

If you know your topic well and know who your audience is, it is possible to anticipate most of the questions that will be asked. When preparing your presentation, always try to make a list of questions you expect to be asked. Some of the most common questions will be something like:

What has to be done?	How long does it take?
How much does it cost?	Is there a deadline?
What are the alternatives?	Do we get support?
Who will be responsible?	What can go wrong?

6 Work with a partner. First think of a topic you both know well (eg an update on a current project or plans for a new project). Work separately to write four or five questions about the topic. Then use the flow chart to practise asking and answering your questions.

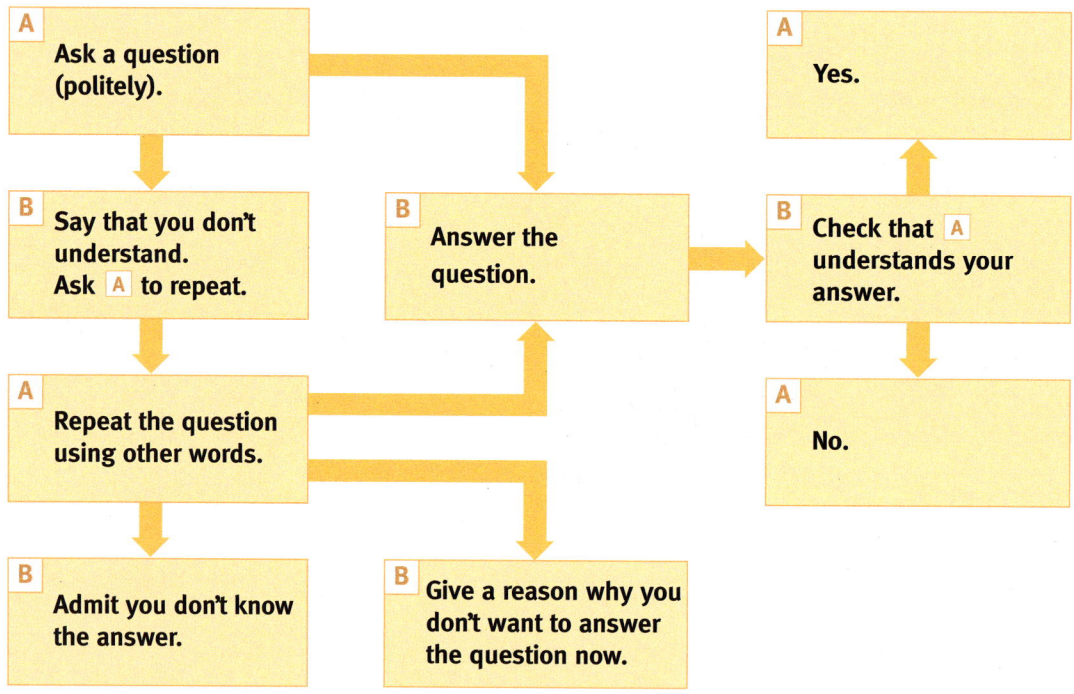

7 Sometimes you have to deal with interruptions or unexpected questions during your presentation. Listen to the following excerpts from four different presentations and say in which one the presenter ...

43–46

a postpones answering the question. ☐

b deals with an aggressive question. ☐

c explains a term that somebody doesn't understand. ☐

d deals with a difficult question. ☐

8   **Now listen again and complete the sentences the presenters use to deal with the interruptions.**

43–46

1   _____ is how we can

meet the delivery date as we are slightly under-staffed in production at the moment.

2   Sorry, _____

when we discuss the financial side of this merger. OK, I was just moving on to the timing of the

merger and …

3   Yes, _____ . Let me just _____

_____ so that everybody can hear.

4   Yes, sure. _____ big credit card companies … use special microchips

instead of the usual magnetic strips on their cards. _____

your question?

DEALING WITH INTERRUPTIONS

Sometimes you may be asked questions during the presentation, even if you have asked the
audience to wait. Whereas some questions can and should be answered quickly (for example, when
a participant hasn't understood something you've said), you might prefer to postpone unwelcome
questions or comments.

> If you don't mind, I'll deal with this question later in my presentation.
> Can we get back to that a bit later?
> Would you mind waiting with your questions until the question and answer session at the end?

After answering questions, especially those that require a longer answer, it is sometimes necessary
to remind the audience what you were talking about before the interruption.

> Before we continue, let me briefly summarize the points we were discussing.
> So, back to what I was saying about …

---

9   **Complete the gaps with verbs from the box. Sometimes more than one answer is possible.**

answer • deal • go • mention • mind • move • prefer • recap • summarize

1   Well, actually, I'd _____ to answer your question after the presentation.

2   To _____ what we were discussing, let me _____ the following points.

3   Sorry, but I'd rather not _____ with this question now as we'll be looking at that in

detail later on this morning.

4   Let me just _____ back to what we were discussing earlier.

5   I'll _____ this question in the course of my presentation.

6   Before we _____ on, let me briefly _____ the main points we have been

talking about.

7   I'm sorry, but would you _____ waiting until the question period?

REFORMULATING QUESTIONS

It is sometimes necessary to reformulate a question (ie say it in another way) before answering it. This not only gives you time to think, it also allows you to make sure you have understood the question. With a large or noisy audience, it allows the other participants to hear the question (again) and finally, it gives you the chance to change the tone of the question, eg by making it less aggressive.

You can use the following phrases and the techniques in the table below to reformulate questions:

I see. So, what you're asking is: …
If I understand you correctly, you want to know …
OK, let me just repeat your question so everybody can hear it.
If I could just rephrase your question …

The question is …	You reformulate to make it …	by …
negative *Isn't there a better solution?*	positive *What would be a better solution?*	leaving out negative words such as 'no', 'never', 'none'
aggressive *Do you honestly believe* *we can get the contract?*	neutral *You're asking whether I think* *it is possible to get the contract.*	avoiding words which sound aggressive or have a negative meaning such as 'honestly', 'really', 'disaster'

---

10 **Reformulate the following questions using the techniques and phrases in the box above.**

1 Are you really sure we can meet our deadline?
2 Won't we get support from headquarters?
3 Do you really think this will work?

4 Do you honestly think we can rely on them?
5 Isn't there a better way to reduce costs?

11 **Translate these sentences. Try to use expressions from this unit.**

1 Wenn ich Sie richtig verstehe, möchten Sie wissen, wie das System funktioniert.
2 Diese Frage kann ich leider nicht beantworten.
3 Vielleicht können wir diesen Punkt bei anderer Gelegenheit besprechen.
4 Mich würde interessieren, ob wir die Frist einhalten können.
5 Darf ich Sie fragen, wie Sie zu diesen Zahlen gekommen sind?
6 Ich schlage vor, Sie sprechen mit Frau Sauer aus der Marketingabteilung.

12 **It's your turn now. Practise the phrases from this unit using the checklist.**

CHECKLIST FOR QUESTIONS

☑ 1 Listen carefully.
☑ 2 Make sure you have understood the question correctly.
☑ 3 Reformulate the question in your own words.
☑ 4 If you want to postpone the question, say why politely.
☑ 5 If you don't know the answer, say so and offer to find out.
☑ 6 Answer irrelevant questions politely but briefly.
☑ 7 Check that the questioner is satisfied with your answer.

Look at what these people say about the question and answer session.
Which opinion(s) do you agree with?

> **Person 1:** *For me, the question and answer session is the most difficult part of a presentation. I don't like it at all. You never know what questions will be asked, so you can't really prepare. I always feel extremely nervous. The problem is you have to say something quickly and don't have the time to think of a clever reply.*

> **Person 2** *If you ask me, most questions aren't really questions at all. It seems as if a lot of people ask questions not because they want to get an answer but because they want to show the other participants how clever they are or how funny or whatever. I think some people just want to show off or be the centre of attention.*

> **Person 3** *I like the way questions are asked by American audiences. My experience is that they usually say something positive about a presentation before they start asking questions. I think that's a very good thing because the questioner shows some respect for the presenter and also helps create a more relaxed and friendly atmosphere during the question period.*

> **Person 4** *I think it's important to try and predict all the questions you might be asked. Before a presentation I always make a list of questions I expect people to ask. Then I think about possible answers and practise them. Sometimes I even get friends and colleagues to ask me questions. Of course you can't anticipate all the questions but at least you don't need to worry about the ones you have thought about. I feel much more comfortable this way.*

> **Person 5** *You need to decide when you want to answer questions. Allowing questions during your talk usually creates a rather informal, seminar-like atmosphere. You can answer questions directly and involve the audience. On the other hand, answering questions after the presentation gives you more control of your structure and timing. If you want questions after your talk, you can say that your time frame is very tight or the topic is rather complex.*

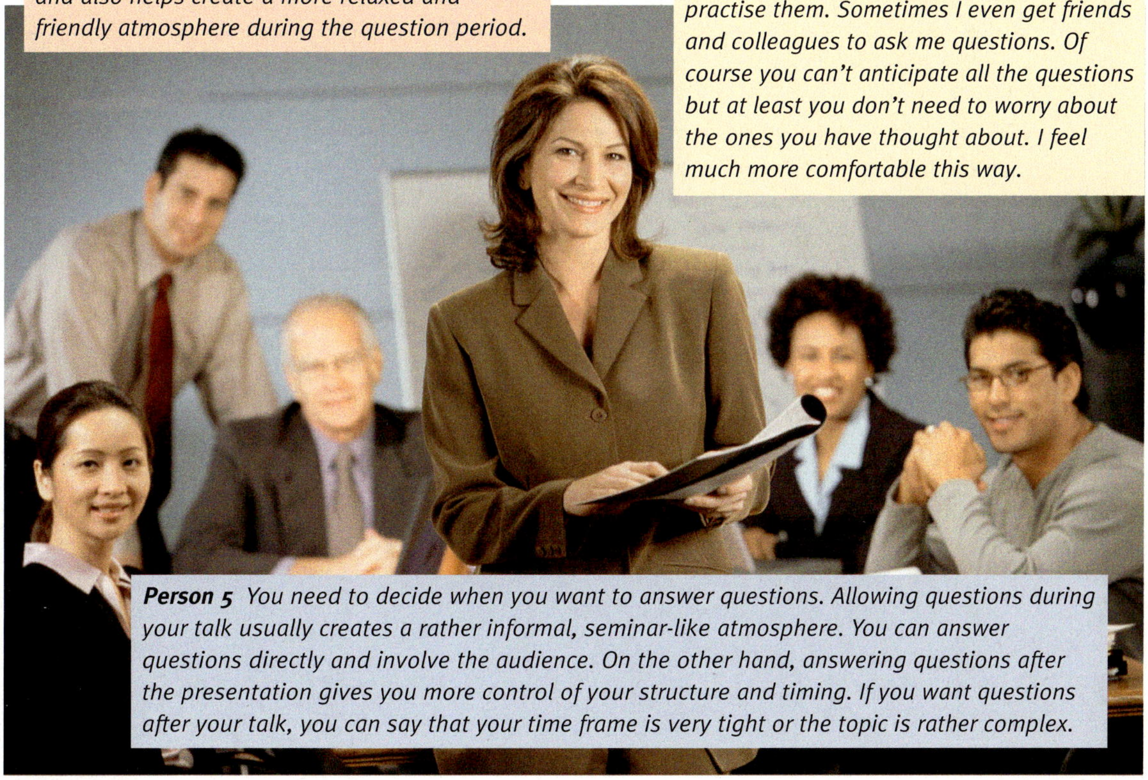

Over to you

Do you usually answer questions during or after your talk? Which do you prefer?

What other tips can you think of for preparing for the question period?

How often do you present to an English-speaking audience? How different is it from presenting to a German-speaking one?

Test yourself!

See how much you've learned about giving presentations in English.
Use the clues to complete the crossword.

Across

2   'als Erstes': *... of all, I'd like to talk about the new project.*

4   'unterbrechen': *If you have any questions, please feel free to ... me at any time.*

10 The opposite of 'increase': *We have experienced a drastic ... in orders.*

13 'schwanken': *Orders generally ... between 1.2 and 1.4 million.*

15 Indicating the end of one section and the start of the next: *This ... me directly to my next topic.*

16 Written material for the audience: *I've prepared a ... for you.*

17 'in few words': *Let me just go over this again ... .*

21 Another word for 'approaching': *I'm ... the end of my talk today.*

22 'zusammenfassen': *Let me ... the main issues.*

23 Another word for 'said': *As I ... earlier, the situation is improving.*

26 'very small': *There has been a ... decrease in sales this year.*

27 *If you don't mind, I'd ... not to discuss this today.*

29 Another word for 'part'.

30 'erhöhen': *The British government has ... taxes again this year.*

31 'sich vorstellen': *Let me ... myself. My name is ... .*

Down

1   What's the preposition? *She is the regional manager, responsible ... Europe.*

3   'Präsentationsfolie' (PowerPoint): *Let's look at the next ... .*

5   A good visual for showing percentages.

6   To deal with something (like a question) later.

7   Another word for 'emphasize': *I'd like to ... the main advantages.*

8   'Thema': *As you know, today's ... is market segmentation.*

9   'Zahlen': *Here you can see the sales ... for 2005.*

11 To repeat the same question or information in a different way.

12 'Tabelle': *This ... gives us an overview of the situation.*

14 A polite way of asking somebody to do something. *Would you ... repeating that?*

18 Another way to say 'regarding': *With ... to.*

19 To make sure something is clear.

20 What's the preposition? *If we don't do something, we will run ... serious financial trouble.*

24 'betonen': *Let me ... the fact that we need to act quickly.*

25 A general description of the most important facts: *I'll begin by giving you an ... .*

28 Another word for 'role': *I am here in my ... as head of marketing.*

Answer key

UNIT 1

page 5

1 **Presentation 1**
Klaus Scherbaum
head of logistics
new semi-automatic shelving system
people who place orders

Presentation 2
–

–
project documentation
people involved in international project management

Presentation 3
Susan Webster
human resources manager
in-company training and qualification programmes
department heads

Formal   1, 3
Less formal   2

page 6

2 1 First of all
2 introduce
3 present
4 particularly; place orders
5 make it; notice
6 screen; topic
7 important; involved
8 aware; schedules
9 probably; human resources
10 department heads; I'll need

3 a 3, 6   b 1, 5, 8   c 2, 9   d 4, 7, 10

order: b – c – a – d

page 7

4 1 Hi, everyone.
2 What I want to do today is …
3 As you know, I'm …
4 It's good to see you all here.
5 In my talk I'll tell you about …
6 Today I'm going to talk about …
7 OK, shall we get started?
8 I know you are all very busy …

page 8

6 2 *showing* you how the database works.
3 talking about EU tax reform.
4 bring you up to date on SEKO's investment plans.
5 report on our financial targets for the division.
6 update you on the proposed training project.
7 looking at business opportunities in Asia.
8 begin by telling you what Jane's group is working on.

page 9

7 1 start   3 Finally   5 all   7 areas
2 Then   4 divided   6 After   8 third

8 1 for   3 of   5 on   7 about
2 into   4 at   6 with   8 to

page 10

9 1 d   5 c   9 h
2 f   6 g   10 j
3 b   7 e
4 a   8 i

B – D – I – F – G – A – C – H – E

page 11

10 2 sections   5 responsible for
3 I'm   6 realize
4 After that; turn

11 1 c   3 h   5 b   7 a
2 d   4 g   6 f   8 e

page 12

12 a 4   b 3   c 1   d 2

1 You know; came across; magazines
2 Imagine; responsible; go about it
3 Did you know that
4 asking you a question; tell you why

13 1 Did you know that American Airlines saved $40,000 in 1987 by eliminating one olive from each salad served in first-class?
2 I read in an article somewhere that 'can't' is a four-letter word. I tend to agree with that!
3 Imagine you won a million euros. Who would you tell first?
4 Can we really compete with the Chinese? Of course we can!

page 13

14 (suggested answers)
1 OK, shall we get started?/OK, let's start.
2 The subject/topic of my presentation today is customer satisfaction.
3 My presentation should/will take about 30 minutes.
4 I'll focus on three issues/points.
5 We will start by looking at the current status of the project.
6 Did you know that this car is very popular in China?

15 1 i   2 a   3 c   4 g   5 d   6 h
7 f   8 b   9 e

UNIT 2

page 15

First of all ...
(suggested answers)
1 b   2 c   3 b/c   4 a   5 a/c
6 a   7 a/c

1 short-time work   3
insurance market   2
handbooks   1
transport regulations   4

- informing the audience about something: 2, 4
- suggesting some solutions to a problem: 1, 3

page 16

2 1 I'd like to do
2 purpose; major developments
3 want to do
4 objective

3 1 The purpose **of** my talk today is **to** update you **on** new developments **in** R&D.
2 What I want to do is **to** present alternatives **to** existing booking procedures.
3 My aim is **to** show you how **to** cut costs **in** IT support.
4 The objective of my presentation is **to** give you an overview **of** the British job market.
5 Our goal is **to** determine our sales targets **for** next year.
6 I am here today **to** report **on** my/our company's investment plans.

4 1 c   2 a   3 b   4 e   5 d

page 17

1 so that's   6 my next point
2 let's move on   7 So much for
3 As I said earlier   8 Let's now turn
4 I'd like to tell   9 what I said earlier.
5 let me give you

page 18

5 2 So, let me first give you a brief overview ...
3 This now leads us to my next point.
4 Let's move on to the next point.
5 Let's now turn to the next issue.
6 So much for ...
7 So that's the background ...
8 As I said earlier ...
9 Let me now come back to what I said earlier.

6 2 This brings us directly to my next question.
3 This leads to the next point, which is price.
4 Let's turn now to the issue of customer service.
5 As I mentioned before, I'd like to give you a brief overview of our activities.
6 I'd like to come back to this question later.
7 Let's go back to what we were discussing earlier.
8 As I said earlier, I'll be focussing on our new sales strategies.

page 19

7 1 main points   5 covered
2 discussing   6 wanted
3 inform   7 leads
4 sum up   8 back

8 (suggested answers)
2 As you already know, Tony Dale is our new marketing manager for print media.
3 As I said at the beginning of my talk, we can't operate from our local airport because we have no permission/not been given permission.
4 As I explained ten minutes ago, we have to choose between two options.
5 As you can see on the slide, sales have increased by 10% since the beginning of the year.

9 1 True
2 False: There are only problems with supply and distribution.
3 True
4 False: They have had to return around 40% of the bottles.
5 False: They may have trouble with their Christmas business.

page 20

10 1 are ... having   5 prevent
2 identify   6 accept
3 deal   7 don't solve
4 cope   8 will ('ll) run

page 21

11 1 deal   4 take care
2 cope   5 solve
3 identify   6 clarify

12 1 with regard   4 Apart from
2 Moreover   5 regarding
3 concerns   6 According to

13 (suggested answers)
1 Let's now turn to/move on to the next point.
2 As you all know, our topic today/today's topic is globalization.
3 My aim is to inform you of/about the latest developments.
4 Additionally/In addition to this, we will discuss/be discussing the most important figures.
5 As I mentioned before/As I said earlier, I'd like to give you/I'll give you a short/brief overview.
6 According to this study, our customers are satisfied with it.

UNIT 3

page 23

First of all ...
1 microphone   6 screen
2 markers   7 OHP
3 whiteboard   8 transparency
4 flip chart   9 pointer
5 data projector   10 pin board

1 Flip chart 3
Whiteboard 1
PowerPoint slide 2

page 24

2 1 these figures
   2 highlight; two quarters
   3 figures; board
   4 have a look
   5 next slide; illustration
   6 sales figures; first
   7 can see
   8 go back; page
   9 flip back

3 1 h   2 c   3 a   4 g   5 d   6 e
   7 b   8 f

page 25

4 1 Two hundred and fifty-one
   2 Seven thousand, four hundred and eighty-nine
   3 Three point eight billion
   4 Forty-nine million euro(s)
   5 Nineteen dollars and sixty-two cents
   6 Two-thirds
   7 One hundred and seventy-five square metres
   8 One million, two hundred and forty thousand
   9 Seven point two

5 1 18,250   5 400 m^2
   2 47,500   6 €239
   3 8,350   7 €215
   4 24.8 m

page 26

6 **– (less)**   **+/– (about the same)**   **+ (more)**
   a little less than   about; almost   just over
   just under   approximately   well over
                             around; nearly
                             roughly

(suggested answers)
2 Almost/Nearly 15%
3 roughly two million euro(s)
4 just over/approximately 18° centigrade
5 just under/a little less than four dollars
6 approximately/roughly 400 square meters

page 27

8 (suggested answers)
   1 **Design/Unique design/Refrigerator design**
      • more colourful
        – customers can change colours
        – five colours to choose from
      • circular shelving system
      • compact design

   2 **Survey: British Businesses and the Euro**
      • 49% 'wait and see'
      • 13% never
      • 35% yes, immediately

   1 turn to the next point
   2 I'd like to draw your attention
   3 What's really interesting here
   4 are the results of this survey?; extremely interesting
   5 The really good news is that
   6 So, where do we go from here?

page 28

9 1 e   2 g   3 b   4 a   5 c   6 d
   7 h   8 f

10 1 extremely dangerous   5 completely useless
    2 absolutely necessary   6 absolutely safe
    3 highly interesting   7 incredibly cheap
    4 surprisingly good

page 29

11 1 draw your attention   5 On the other hand
    2 you will see   6 can we explain
    3 The figures also show that 7 have a look
    4 It is quite remarkable   8 let's talk about

12 **Making contrasts**   **Describing results**
    Although   As a result
    Despite   Consequently
    However   Therefore
    Nevertheless   Thus
    On the other hand
    Whereas
    While

page 30

    1 however   4 Despite
    2 Although   5 Consequently
    3 Whereas   6 On the other hand

13 (suggested answers)
    1 Let's now have a closer look at this table.
    2 On the next transparency/slide you can see the sales figures for the first quarter.
    3 We sell almost/nearly 30% of our products to other European countries.
    4 I'd like to draw your attention to the following facts.
    5 Despite software problems we were able to achieve surprisingly good results.
    6 I'd like to emphasize/stress how important this change is/the importance of this change.

UNIT 4

page 32

First of all ...
bar chart   1   map   5
table   3   pie chart   4
technical drawing   8   organigram   6
flow chart   7   (line) graph   2

a pie chart
b flow chart
c organigram

page 33

1 Presentation 1: pie chart
   Presentation 2: (line) graph
   Presentation 3: bar chart

   1 chart; breakdown
   2 segment; percentage
   3 have a look
   4 left-hand; represents
   5 draw
   6 take a look; slide
   7 bar chart; left; per cent

2 1 B 2 A 3 D 4 E 5 F 6 C
7 H 8 G

page 34

3 1 C 2 F 3 I 4 E 5 A
6 H 7 J 8 G 9 B 10 D

4
1 divided	5 surprised
2 shown	6 amount
3 see	7 attention
4 total	8 account

page 35

5

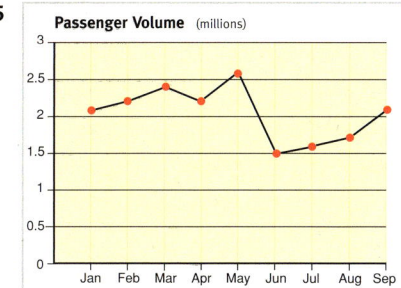

Passenger Volume (millions)

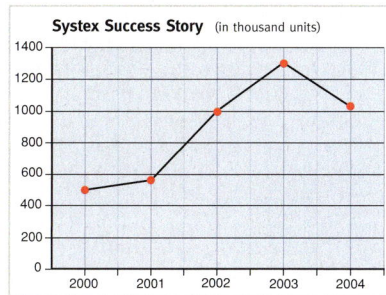

Systex Success Story (in thousand units)

6 **Presentation 1**
1 fluctuated
2 rose
3 fall
4 slumped; decline
5 picking up
6 reached

Presentation 2
1 rose
2 rocketed
3 increase
4 went down; stood

page 36

7
Upward	Downward	Other
climb	decline	fluctuate
double	decrease	remain stable
expand	drop	stabilize
go up	fall	stay the same
grow	go down	
increase	hit a low	
pick up	plunge	
reach a high		
recover		
rise		

page 37

8 2 Sales dropped at the beginning of the year.
3 Energy consumption has increased over the past 30 years.
4 Gas prices went up last month.
5 The number of customers has grown since 2004.
6 Surprisingly, interest rates fell yesterday.

7 TBN's share price hit a low after the crash in 1999.
8 Online bookings have doubled since May last year.
9 Order volumes fluctuated between May and July.

(suggested answers)
2 Sales increased/rose at the beginning of the year.
3 Energy consumption has decreased/declined over the past 30 years.
4 Gas prices went down/fell last month.
5 The number of customers has fallen/decreased since 2004.
6 Surprisingly, interest rates rose/went up yesterday.

9 1 Correct
2 Incorrect: Unemployment rose …
3 Incorrect: Why did they raise …
4 Correct
5 Incorrect: Interest rates will rise …
6 Incorrect: The company raised …

page 38

10
1 fell	4 has grown
2 has improved	5 have doubled
3 plunged	6 slumped

11 1 c 2 e 3 g 4 a 5 d
6 f 7 b

drastic decline
improve significantly
rise steadily
temporary setback

page 39

12 (suggested answers)
2 fell dramatically
3 have declined slightly
4 rose sharply
5 has grown considerably
6 has decreased steadily

13 (suggested answers)
2 This was followed by a sharp fall in income.
3 We have seen a drastic decline in the number of jobs this year.
4 There was a slight drop in hotel rates in Munich.
5 This was followed by a sudden increase in tourist numbers.
6 There has been a steady growth in social security costs.

page 40

14 1 There are several reasons for the decrease in productivity.
2 We chose this method because we needed reliable figures.
3 The result of this move was a drastic increase in our costs.
4 Our new policy has led to a significant rise in sales.
5 The slump was caused by the collapse of one of our partner firms.
6 Downsizing resulted in a drastic fall in staff numbers.

7 We increased our prices and our sales went up!
8 Our output has doubled thanks to a new overtime policy.

cause: 1, 2, 5   effect: 3, 4, 6, 7, 8

15 1 in
2 between
3 to
4 until
5 from
6 of
7 around
8 by
9 at

16 (suggested answers)
1 The pie chart shows our market share in per cent/percentage of the market share.
2 According to the study, travel costs have risen sharply/dramatically since 2000.
3 Interest rates were raised by 0.5% at the beginning of the year.
4 In June, there was a dramatic rise of 15% in transport costs.
5 Our productivity hit a low in December.
6 The decline/slump was caused by the poor economic situation./The reason for the decline/slump was the poor economic situation.

UNIT 5

page 42

1 1 To find out whether they can reduce air travel costs by using budget airlines and if so, how to proceed.
2 The options are: to take on a part-time employee, to have staff book their own flights or to outsource the function.
3 The best solution is to employ a part-timer.
4 The presenter recommends that the ideal candidate either has Internet experience or has previously worked for a travel agent.

page 43

2 Signalling the end of the presentation
Well, this brings me to the end of my presentation. (6)
Thank you all for listening. (a)
OK, I think that's everything I wanted to say ... (e)
As a final point, I'd like to ... (h)
I'm now nearing the end of my talk ... (i)

Summarizing the main points
I'll just run through the three different options. (1)
Before I stop let me go through the main points again. (5)
To sum up then, we ... (d)
I'd like to run through my main points again ... (g)
Just to summarize the main points of my talk ... (j)

Recommending or suggesting something
We'd suggest ... (2)
We'd therefore recommend that we ... (4)
In my opinion, we should ... (b)
What I'd like to suggest is ... (k)

Inviting questions
Now I'll be happy to answer any questions you may have. (3)
We just have time for a few questions. (b)
Are there any questions? (f)

page 44

3 1 Well, that brings me to the end of my talk today.
2 Before I stop, let me go over the key issues again.
3 As a final point, let me say what this means for us.
4 Finally, I'd like to highlight one key issue.
5 To sum up then, we first looked at the product range ...
6 That covers just about everything I wanted to say about logistics.

4 1 briefly summarize
2 figures we have
3 now approaching
4 to highlight
5 final point
6 my opinion
7 come back
8 suggest that

page 45

5 (model answer)
I'm now nearing the end of my talk. I'd just like to run through the main points again. First I talked about the delays that we've been having with the first trials and showed you how we are dealing with them. Then we reviewed the various partners that are currently involved in the project and how we can work together most effectively. Finally, I talked about the next steps, ie where we go from here. So, to conclude, I'd like to highlight one key point. That's the fact that we were able to get IRG Design involved. This is very important to the success of the project as they have a lot of experience in this area and a very good reputation for quality. So, now you've got the full picture. Any questions?

6 Call to action 4   Question 2
Story   1   Quotation 3

a Presentation 2: do we really want to miss
b Presentation 3: finish with something
c Presentation 4: So, the next step is yours
d Presentation 1: Let me go back to the story; Remember; So, this just shows you

page 46

7 1 f   2 b   3 e   4 g   5 c
6 a   7 d

8 1 on
2 In
3 to
4 for
5 through
6 out
7 about
8 by

9 **Across**
4 quote
5 suggest
6 highlight
9 recap
10 all

Down
1 through
2 cons
3 key
7 goal
8 track

page 47

10 3 never
4 We
5 us
6 strategy
7 dramatic
8 production
9 I
10 start

page 48

11 Finally, // let me come back to the <u>key points</u> of my talk. // I told you that in the first quarter, // more than <u>half</u>, or <u>52%</u>, // of eBay's revenues // came from overseas. // This is <u>in line</u> with the targets we set out // in <u>2004</u> // when we decided we wanted to <u>continue</u> to rely on overseas markets, // <u>especially</u> China, to keep growing. In the <u>past</u> three months we've added <u>more</u> new users in China // than in <u>any</u> other country.
<u>Now</u> // what are our targets for the <u>next</u> few months? // The <u>first</u> major step // will be the introduction of our <u>PayPal</u> payment service in China. // And <u>then</u> // we will focus on finding customers in <u>existing</u> markets, // such as the <u>US</u> and <u>Germany</u>, // who <u>haven't</u> tried buying or selling on eBay yet.

12 (suggested answers)
1 Let me summarize the most important results.
2 I'd like to go through the main points again.
3 In my opinion, we have to / must change our sales strategy.
4 I'd recommend that we focus / concentrate on the German market.
5 I'm now nearing / approaching the end of my talk / presentation.
6 Now let's put it into practice!

UNIT 6

page 50

1 She answers the question: 1
She doesn't answer: 3
She doesn't know the answer: 4
She doesn't understand the question: 2

page 51

2 1 happy to
2 do you mean
3 mentioned earlier
4 Would you mind
5 quite understand
6 another question
7 don't mind
8 Actually
9 Could you tell us
10 I'm afraid; could answer

page 52

3 1 d   2 b   3 a   4 f   5 g
6 i   7 c   8 h   9 e

a: 3, 6, 9
b: 1, 2
c: 4, 5, 7, 8

4 1 Are there any questions?
2 Could you give us
3 Would you mind
4 No, not at all.
5 May I ask
6 Go ahead.
7 I'd be interested
8 I suggest you speak to
9 Excuse me.
10 Does that mean

page 53

5 3 how we compare with other firms?
4 whether we will cooperate with other branches in the UK?

5 how she arrived at those results?
6 if / whether there are any figures to back this up?

1 a   2 b   3 e   4 c   5 f   6 d

page 54

7 a 2   b 1   c 4   d 3

8 1 If I have understood you correctly, Louise, your question
2 if you don't mind, I'd like to answer your question a bit later
3 that is a very valid question; repeat it
4 It means that; Does that answer

9 1 prefer
2 summarize / recap; mention
3 deal
4 go
5 answer
6 move; summarize / recap
7 mind

page 56

10 (suggested answers)
1 I see, so what you're asking is: How can we be sure to meet the deadline?
2 If I understand you correctly, you want to know whether we will get support from headquarters.
3 If I could just rephrase your question, you'd like to know how this will work.
4 You're asking me whether we can rely on them.
5 OK, let me just rephrase your question so everybody can hear it. You want to know the most effective way to reduce costs.

11 (suggested answers)
1 If I have understood you correctly, you would like to know how the system works.
2 I'm afraid I can't answer that question.
3 Perhaps we can get back to that point later.
4 I'd be interested to know if we can meet the deadline.
5 May I ask how you arrived at those figures?
6 I suggest you speak to Ms Sauer from the marketing department.

pages 58 / 59

Test yourself!

Across		Down	
2	first	1	for
4	interrupt	3	slide
10	decrease	5	pie chart
13	fluctuate	6	postpone
15	leads	7	highlight
16	handout	8	topic
17	briefly	9	figures
21	nearing	11	rephrase
22	summarize	12	table
23	mentioned	14	mind
26	slight	18	regard
27	prefer	19	clarify
29	section	20	into
30	raised	24	emphasize
31	introduce	25	overview
		28	function

Transcripts

Presentation 1

2 Good morning, ladies and gentlemen. First of all, let me thank you all for being here today. I'm glad that so many of you could come, especially since I know that this time of the year is probably the busiest for you. Let me introduce myself. My name is Klaus Scherbaum. I'm the head of logistics here at Air Spares, Hamburg. Logistics is a centre of competency dedicated to providing you with the spare parts you need, precisely when you need them. I'm here today to present our new semi-automatic shelving system. My talk is particularly relevant to those of you who place orders for the different parts we supply.

Presentation 2

3 OK, shall we get started? Hello everyone. I'm happy that so many of you could make it today at such short notice. I know that you're all extremely busy at the moment, so I'd like to start with my presentation right away. As you can see on the screen, our topic today is project documentation. We're going to look closely at drafting, storing, archiving as well as accessing documents in our new SAP system. We'll also examine the much improved handling of all project document-ation as well as user rights. This is extremely important for all of us who are directly involved in international project management, right? You don't need me to spell it out ... if it isn't documented, it doesn't exist.

Presentation 3

4 Good afternoon. I'm aware that you all have very tight schedules, so I appreciate you taking the time to come here today. As you probably know, my name is Susan Webster. I'm the new human resources manager here at Weston Ltd. What I'd like to present to you today is my department's new concept for improving our in-company training and qualification programmes. This is based on feedback from your departments. Today's topic will be very important for you as department heads, since I'll need your help to evaluate and select candidates for training.

1

6 You know, I was sitting in the waiting room at the dentist's the other day when I came across something very interesting in one of the magazines that was lying there. It said that chocolate is really a vegetable because we get it from cocoa and sugar which come from cocoa beans and sugar cane – both plants, ie vegetables, right? Chocolate a health food? Ha! You know, it's all about the way things are presented and how we look at them. Image building, ladies and gentlemen, that is our business and we're here today to ...

2

7 Imagine you worked in a small to medium-sized company and were responsible for making people in your company aware of health and safety issues. How would you go about it? Would you have a meeting? Send everyone an email? Take a few moments to think about it.

3

8 Did you know that the number of possible ways of playing the first four moves per side in a game of chess is 318,979,564,000? Let me just write that number on the board: 318 billion, 979 million and 564 thousand. Now, what does that have to do with our topic today, which, as you know, is project management? Well, let me tell you.

4

9 So, let me start by asking you a question. Why should we introduce a double quality check here at Auto Spares & Parts, one at goods-in and another at goods-out? After all, our products come from certified suppliers and we have an excellent track record for providing quick and competent service. So, why bother? Well, I'm here today to tell you why. For those of you who don't know me, my name is ...

1

10 As you know, I've been asked to talk to you about the handbooks for our all-in-one systems for smaller businesses. Peter Collins from customer care has told me that they have been getting a lot of phone calls and emails from users who say that the set-up instructions are extremely complicated and don't match the sketches. What I'd like to do today is to make some suggestions on how we can make our handbooks more user-friendly.

2

11 I'd like to talk to you today about how globalization has changed the face of the insurance industry. The purpose of my talk is to provide you with information on the major developments in the insurance market in the last few months. I'd like to start with ...

3

12 OK, let's get started. We're here to discuss the introduction of short-time work in our company. As you know, our order books are not the fullest at the moment so we have to find ways to get through this crisis and at the same time keep jobs. What I want to do this morning is to show you how we could reorganize our working hours. Among other things, I'll be talking about ...

4

13 As you can see from your handouts, we'll be looking at some new European transport regulations today. The objective is to bring you up to date with the latest changes which will be introduced on January 1. These changes will mainly affect transport companies in the EU but they will also ...

UNIT 2, EXERCISE 9

15 Thanks, Jim. OK. As you probably know, we are currently having difficulties with our new men's cosmetic line. These problems lie chiefly with our main bottle supplier, but we are also having trouble with distribution. I'd like to quickly identify the problems and then make some suggestions on how we can deal with the consequences.

So let's start with our bottle supplier then … . We've been having serious difficulties with GSG, which is our main plastic bottle supplier, regarding both quantity and quality. We don't understand why, but they don't seem to be able to supply the quantities we order from them. In addition, the quality of the material is so poor that we have had to return about 40% of the bottles. We've been trying to cope with these problems – the delays, the poor quality – all along, but so far we've not been able to find ways to prevent them from happening again. It's clear we can no longer continue to accept these conditions. Moreover, we're now getting ready for the Christmas season. If we don't solve our supply problems within the next two weeks, we'll run into serious trouble with respect to our Christmas business.

Let's move on to distribution. Here the problem lies with …

UNIT 3, EXERCISE 1

16 **1**
Take a look at these figures. They clearly highlight how a combination of two significant external factors affected our business in the first two quarters of this year. One important factor is the oil price, the second the development of the euro against the dollar. In 2002 we exported nearly two-thirds of our products to the US and Canada. Since then oil has become much more expensive and so has the euro. Let me show you what this means for our export business. I'll just write some figures on the board and then we will go on to discuss the next point.

17 **2**
OK. Let's now have a look at our new magnetic ski rack Matterhorn which was launched in August. This system is more compact than the old one and also easier to handle. Another advantage is that it can also be used for snowboards. We hope to sell at least 5,000 of these systems within the next two months. On the next slide you will see an illustration of the Matterhorn X-15.

18 **3**
As I explained earlier, we've worked very hard to make our products more attractive for the customer. These are the sales figures for Germany for the first three quarters of this year. As you can see here, we've had a very successful year. We have sold about 21,000 fully automatic espresso machines and nearly 7,500 semi-automatic machines so far. To highlight our success even further, let's go back to the 2003 figures on the previous page. Let me just flip back to it. Ah yes, here it is.

UNIT 3, EXERCISE 5

20 **1**
Let's look at the figures in this table more closely. As you can see in the first row, we sold 18,250 cars in Germany in the first quarter while in the same period we sold roughly 32,000 in the EU. Our non-EU market was still relatively small with sales of about 8,000 cars. Now if you look at the second quarter, you will see a dramatic change. Whereas our German business didn't increase much, sales in the other two areas developed very well. In the EU, 47,500 cars were sold and in non-EU countries sales went up to 17,300, which I'm sure you will agree is an extremely good result.

21 **2**
If you look at the next slide, you will see the layout of our new open-plan office in Hamburg. As you can see from the plan, it's 24.8 metres long and about 16 metres wide, for a total of just over 400 square metres. Our office will be on the 12th floor of the building, which has a total of 16 floors. We will be moving to our new premises on 15 February if everything goes according to plan.

22 **3**
You can see the five most expensive cities for business travellers in this table. Venice leads the table with an average rate of €387. In Rome, the business traveller has to pay €239 and in Paris a room costs €226. In New York City the average room rate is €225 and in Milan it's €215 per night.

UNIT 3, EXERCISE 8

23 **1**
So, we've seen that our new line of refrigerators is environmentally friendly. Let's now turn to the next point, which is their unique design. I'd like to draw your attention to three new design features. First, the refrigerators are more colourful. Apple started the trend of colourful computers in the office. We think that consumers want more colour in their kitchens, too, and our refrigerators provide that. What's really interesting here is that customers can change the colour panels – there are five colours to choose from – to match their home, their mood, the seasons, whatever. The second unique design feature is the circular shelving system. Each shelf can be rotated, so that all items of food are easy to reach and nothing gets lost in the back of the fridge again. And finally, the new refrigerator has a compact design. This means that it takes up less floor space while holding as much as a conventional refrigerator.

24 **2**
About 1,000 businesses in the UK were asked if Britain should introduce the euro. What are the results of this survey? Well, I think you'll agree that the results are quite interesting. As you can see from this table, 49% said they wanted to 'wait and see'. Only 13% said Britain should never join the euro zone. The good news is that nearly 35% said we should go in immediately. So, where do we go from here?

UNIT 4, EXERCISE 1

Presentation 1

26 The next chart shows the breakdown by age in our company. You can see that the biggest segment – almost 70% – indicates the percentage of employees in the age group 35 to 50. About 19% of our staff are between 51 and 60 years of age and 2% are above 60. The final 'pie' is the most interesting for our discussion today; it shows the percentage of employees under 35 years of age, which I think you'll be surprised to hear is currently only 9% of our total staff.

Presentation 2

27 Let's now have a look at the sales figures over the past five years. First, let me quickly explain the graph. You can see that different colours have been used to indicate each of our main sales areas. The key in the bottom left-hand corner shows you which colour represents which area. The red line, for example, gives us the sales figures for Belgium, the green line is for Germany and so on. OK, so I'd like to first draw your attention to the sales figures for France – that's the blue line here.

Presentation 3

28 Now I'd like you to take a look at this next slide which shows how the cost of living developed in Germany between 2000 and 2004. According to the German Economic Institute, living expenses rose by between 1.1 and 2% each year. If you look at the bar chart on the left, you will see that the highest increase was in 2001 with a rise of 2%.

UNIT 4, EXERCISE 5

Presentation 1

29 First, I'd like you to look at this graph, which shows the ups and downs in our passenger volume over the past nine months. As you can see here, passenger numbers fluctuated between 2.1 and 2.3 million in the first four months. They even rose moderately in May, reaching just over 2.5 million at the end of the month. In June you'll notice a sharp fall in passenger numbers as a direct consequence of HLX's entry into the market. Now as you all know, HLX is a no-frills airline with direct flights to almost all major German cities. Passenger traffic slumped to about 1.5 million – a decline of almost 40%. In early July we introduced a new, more aggressive pricing system to boost sales. As a result, ticket sales started picking up in July. By the end of September passenger numbers had reached just over 2 million.

Presentation 2

30 On the next graph you'll see the sales figures for SYSTEX in the past five years. Let me now highlight the most important facts about our hay fever medication. Despite an intensive advertising campaign, we had a slow start in Germany in 2000, selling 500,000 units in the first twelve months. The figure rose by about 50,000 in the following year. In 2002, however, sales rocketed to 1 million following the breakdown of TC PHARMA, our main competitor in the anti-allergy sector. 2003 saw an even further increase in sales to 1.3 million due to the extremely warm and long summer. As expected, sales went down again in 2004 and stood at just over a million at the end of the year.

UNIT 5, EXERCISE 1

32 Well, this brings me to the end of my presentation. Before I stop, let me go through my main points again. You gave us the brief to find out (a) whether we can reduce our air travel costs by using budget airlines and (b) if so, how we should proceed. So, to sum up ... first question: is it really viable to use these no-frills airlines? Clear answer there! In some cases we can save as much as 60% compared to regular flights. The next question: how to proceed? In other words, who would be able to handle the online bookings most efficiently? I'll just run through the three different options we investigated again: option 1, we take on a part-time employee for this job; option 2, staff book their own flights; option 3, we outsource this function. So, what is the best solution for us? From a financial point of view our results are absolutely clear: option one. A part-timer would be the best, the cheapest and least time-consuming solution. We'd therefore recommend that we recruit a part-time employee who could handle all our online bookings. The ideal candidate should either have some Internet experience or have previously worked for a travel agent. We'd suggest a limited contract to begin with. So, now it's up to you to decide where to go from here. I'm sure you'll make the right choice. Now I'll be happy to answer any questions you may have.

UNIT 5, EXERCISE 6

1

33 Let me go back to the story I told at the start of my talk. Remember, the sales meeting in Vienna with the disappointed Japanese businessmen? Three days later we got an email saying they were going with us after all. So, this just shows you that knowing your entire product range is the key to success.

2

34 So, to conclude, I'm convinced that ICM would be an excellent method to make better use of the knowledge we have. And it would strengthen our market position. So, do we really want to miss this opportunity to get ahead of our competitors?

3

35 Finally, let me highlight the key question once again: do we need a digital telephone system or can we upgrade the existing one? As I've shown in my brief presentation today, we must invest in the new system; an upgrade is just not feasible. I'd just like to finish with something former US president Bill Clinton once said: "You can put wings on a pig, but you don't make it an eagle".

4

36 Before I end my presentation today, I'd like to briefly recap the main reasons for doing business with us. We use state-of-the-art technology. We provide round-the-clock professional customer care. And most important, we customize our products and services to give you what you need when you need it. So the next step is yours. Set up an appointment with our project manager and our SAP consultant and we can work out the Best Practice solutions that suit your business.

UNIT 6, EXERCISE 1

1
38

Presenter	And now I'll be happy to answer any questions you may have. Yes?
Man 1	You were talking about software problems. What exactly do you mean by that?
Presenter	Well, I mentioned earlier that the new software is being tested at the moment. In the trial runs we've had more than 150 bugs so far and at the moment we're not sure how long it will take us to solve all these problems. Does that answer your question?
Man 1	Yes, thank you.

2
39

Presenter	Are there any more questions? Mr Lee?
Man 2	Would you mind telling us whether the new software will help to improve our company's image?
Presenter	I'm afraid I don't quite understand your question. Could you be a bit more specific?
Man 2	Yes, I'd like to know whether we will also use the new software to make our company more attractive for the customer. I'm talking about a new website, interactive applications, and so on.
Presenter	Oh, I see. Yes, well, as I said earlier …

3
40

Man 1	I have another question. It's about the piloting stage. Which division will start piloting the software first?
Presenter	If you don't mind, I'd prefer not to discuss that today. Actually, there will be a meeting next week where that will be decided.

4
41

Presenter	Mr Menzel, you have a question?
Man 3	Yes. You spoke about special training courses earlier. Could you tell us how they will be organized?
Presenter	Sorry, I'm afraid that's not my field. But I'm sure Linda Koll from the training department could answer that question. I'll ask her to get in touch with you on that. Well, if there are no more questions, all that remains for me to do is to wish you a nice evening!

UNIT 6, EXERCISE 7

1
43

Presenter	So, delivery of the units has been set for 15 May. That gives us three months to handle the production and packaging. I'd like to turn now to the …
Woman	Ah, excuse me. Do you really think that's realistic? I mean, three months. What about our staff problems?
Presenter	If I have understood you correctly, Louise, your question is how we can meet the delivery date as we are slightly under-staffed in production at the moment. Well, let me answer your question right away. First of all …

2
44

Presenter	And talking of mergers, don't forget the successful German haircare company, Wella, which was taken over by Procter and Gamble only a few years ago. What we need to discuss is whether it's the right moment for us to consider a merger with Carter Financial Services.
Woman	Could you tell us what their turnover was last year?
Presenter	Sorry, if you don't mind, I'd like to answer your question a bit later when we discuss the financial side of this merger. OK, I was just moving on to the timing of the merger and …

3
45

Presenter	… and this brings me to the most important topic of today's session. Due to our new European harmonization strategy, our complete sales, after-sales and marketing departments will be relocated to Bielefeld by July 2007. Now I know this may come as a shock to most of you but I can guarantee that all the staff affected will be fully supported every step of the way.
Man	Excuse me, but may I ask how you propose to support those people who are tied to *this* location, for example those of us who care for elderly parents or whose children are in a special needs school for example?
Presenter	Yes, that is a very valid question. Let me just repeat it so everybody can hear. You're concerned about staff members who will find it difficult to move away from Hamburg due to family commitments. Yes, well, of course we will not force anyone to move and our works council is working very closely with HR to find the best solutions for everyone. If you look on our intranet …

4
46

Presenter	The main advantages of 'smart' credit cards are …
Man	Sorry to interrupt, but could you explain what 'smart' means in this context?
Presenter	Yes, sure. It means that big credit card companies like Visa and Mastercard use special microchips instead of the usual magnetic strips on their cards. Does that answer your question?
Man	Yes, thank you, Peter.
Presenter	OK, so let's go back to the main advantages of 'smart' credit cards. …

A–Z word list

A

to **access** ['ækses]	zugreifen auf
according to [ə'kɔːdɪŋ tə]	laut, nach
to **achieve** [ə'tʃiːv]	erreichen
actually ['æktʃuəli]	in der Tat, tatsächlich
to **admit** [əd'mɪt]	eingestehen
advantage [əd'vɑːntɪdʒ]	Vorteil
advertisement [əd'vɜːtɪsmənt]	Anzeige
advice [əd'vaɪs]	(guter) Rat, Ratschläge
to **affect** [ə'fekt]	beeinflussen
allergy ['ælədʒi]	Allergie
to **allow** [ə'laʊ]	gestatten
amazing [ə'meɪzɪŋ]	erstaunlich
anecdote ['ænɪkdəʊt]	Anekdote
annual ['ænjuəl]	jährlich
to **anticipate** [æn'tɪsɪpeɪt]	vorwegnehmen, vorausahnen
to **applaud** [ə'plɔːd]	applaudieren
application [ˌæplɪ'keɪʃn]	Anwendung
to **appreciate** [ə'priːʃieɪt]	zu schätzen wissen
to **approach** [ə'prəʊtʃ]	sich nähern
to **archive** ['ɑːkaɪv]	archivieren
around [ə'raʊnd]	ungefähr, etwa
as a result of [əz ə rɪ'zʌlt əv]	als Folge von
as well as [əz 'wel əz]	ebenso wie
at least [ət 'liːst]	wenigstens, zumindest
at short notice [ət ʃɔːt 'nəʊtɪs]	kurzfristig
to **attend** [ə'tend]	teilnehmen (an)
attention [ə'tenʃn]	Aufmerksamkeit
audience ['ɔːdiəns]	Publikum, Zuhörer
average ['ævərɪdʒ]	durchschnittlich, Durchschnitts-
to **avoid** [ə'vɔɪd]	vermeiden
aware (of), to be ~ [bi ə'weər əv]	sich einer Sache bewusst sein

B

back and forth [ˌbæk ənd 'fɔːθ]	hin und her
to **back sth up** [ˌbæk 'ʌp]	etw untermauern
background ['bækgraʊnd]	Hintergrund
bar chart ['bɑː tʃɑːt]	Balkendiagramm
based on ['beɪst ɒn]	basierend auf
be responsible for, to be ~ [bi rɪ'spɒnsəbl fə]	verantwortlich/zuständig sein für
to **benefit** ['benɪfɪt]	profitieren
to **boost** [buːst]	ankurbeln
to **bother** ['bɒðə]	sich die Mühe machen
branch [brɑːntʃ]	Niederlassung
brand [brænd]	Marke
breakdown ['breɪkdaʊn]	Aufteilung, Aufschlüsselung
to **breathe** [briːð]	atmen
bug [bʌg]	(Software-)Fehler
bullet chart ['bʊlɪt tʃɑː t]	Stichwortliste, Auflistung

C

campaign [kæm'peɪn]	Kampagne, Aktion
to **catch** [kætʃ]	mitbekommen, verstehen
certain ['sɜːtn]	bestimmte(r)
chess [tʃes]	Schach
circular ['sɜːkjələ]	Rund-
clarification [ˌklærɪfɪ'keɪʃn]	Erklärung
to **clarify** ['klærəfaɪ]	deutlich machen, (auf)klären
to **climb** [klaɪm]	steigen
common interest [ˌkɒmən 'ɪntrəst]	gemeinsames Interesse
to **compare with** [kəm'peə wɪð]	dastehen im Vergleich mit
compared to [kəm'peəd tə]	verglichen mit
competitiveness [kəm'petətɪvnəs]	Wettbewerbsfähigkeit
competitor [kəm'petɪtə]	Konkurrent/in, Mitbewerber/in
to **complain** [kəm'pleɪn]	sich beschweren
concerning [kən'sɜːnɪŋ]	bezüglich, hinsichtlich
conclude, To ~ [tə kən'kluːd]	Zum Abschluss, Abschließend

connection with, in ~ [ɪn kə'nekʃn wɪð]	im Zusammenhang mit
consequence ['kɒnsɪkwəns]	Folge, Konsequenz
consequently ['kɒnsɪkwəntli]	dementsprechend, infolgedessen
considerably [kən'sɪdərəbli]	beträchtlich
construction site [kən'strʌkʃn saɪt]	Baustelle
consumption [kən'sʌmpʃn]	Verbrauch
conventional [kən'venʃənl]	herkömmlich
convinced [kən'vɪnst]	überzeugt
to **cope with** ['kəʊp wɪð]	fertig werden mit
counterpart ['kaʊntəpɑːt]	Pendant, Gegenüber
course of, in the ~ [ɪn ðə 'kɔːs əv]	im Lauf von
to **cover** ['kʌvə]	behandeln
to **cross your arms** [ˌkrɒs jɔː 'ɑːmz]	die Arme verschränken
current status [ˌkʌrənt 'steɪtəs]	aktueller Stand
current ['kʌrənt]	aktuell
to **customize** ['kʌstəmaɪz]	(dem Kunden) anpassen, maßschneidern

D

to **deal with** ['diːl wɪð]	sich befassen mit
to **decline** [dɪ'klaɪn]	abnehmen, zurückgehen
to **decrease** [dɪ'kriːs]	abnehmen
to **dedicate** ['dedɪkeɪt]	widmen
delay [dɪ'leɪ]	Verspätung, Verzögerung
delighted, to be ~ [bi dɪ'laɪtɪd]	sehr erfreut sein, sich freuen
to **describe** [dɪ'skraɪb]	beschreiben
despite [dɪ'spaɪt]	trotz
development [dɪ'veləpmənt]	Entwicklung
diagram ['daɪəgræm]	Strukturbild, Diagramm
disappointed [ˌdɪsə'pɔɪntɪd]	enttäuscht
to **discuss** [dɪ'skʌs]	besprechen
to **distract** [dɪ'strækt]	ablenken
divided [dɪ'vaɪdɪd]	aufgeteilt
dividend ['dɪvɪdend]	Dividende
division [dɪ'vɪʒn]	Sparte, Abteilung
downsizing ['daʊnsaɪzɪŋ]	Personalabbau
to **draft** [drɑːft]	entwerfen
to **drop** [drɒp]	sinken, zurückgehen

E

eagle ['iːgl]	Adler
to **emphasize** ['emfəsaɪz]	betonen, hervorheben
to **ensure** [ɪn'ʃʊə]	sicherstellen, gewährleisten
enthusiasm [ɪn'θjuːziæzəm]	Begeisterung(sfähigkeit)
entire [ɪn'taɪə]	ganz, vollständig
equipment [ɪ'kwɪpmənt]	Ausstattung, Geräte
to **evaluate** [ɪ'væljueɪt]	bewerten, einstufen
to **exhale** [eks'heɪl]	ausatmen

F

to **face** [feɪs]	konfrontiert sein mit
to **fail to do sth** [feɪl]	es nicht fertigbringen, etw zu tun
familiar with, to be ~ [bi fə'mɪliə wɪð]	vertraut sein mit
family commitments [ˌfæməli kə'mɪtmənts]	familiäre Verpflichtungen
feasible ['fiːzəbl]	machbar
to **feel free to do sth** [fiːl 'friː tə]	sich frei fühlen, etw zu tun
to **find ways to** [faɪnd 'weɪz tə]	Möglichkeiten finden
to **fit** [fɪt]	passen, passend sein
to **flip back** [flɪp 'bæk]	zurückblättern
floor space ['flɔː speɪs]	Nutzfläche
flow chart ['fləʊ tʃɑːt]	Flussdiagramm
to **flow** [fləʊ]	fließen
to **fluctuate** ['flʌktʃueɪt]	schwanken
fortunately ['fɔːtʃənətli]	glücklicherweise, zum Glück

G

to **gather** ['gæðə] — sammeln
to **generate sales** ['dʒenəreɪt] — erzeugen, (Absätze) erzielen
gesture ['dʒestʃə] — Geste
to **get ahead of sb** [get ə'hed əv] — jdn übertreffen
to **get down to sth** [get 'daʊn tə] — etw in Angriff nehmen
to **go according to plan** [gəʊ ə,kɔːdɪŋ tə 'plæn] — nach Plan laufen
to **go ahead with sth** [,gəʊ ə'hed] — mit etw fortfahren
goods [gʊdz] — Ware(n)
guideline ['gaɪdlaɪn] — Richtlinie

H

to **handle** ['hændl] — bewältigen, bearbeiten
hay fever ['heɪ fiːvə] — Heuschnupfen
headline ['hedlaɪn] — Schlagzeile
headquarters [,hed'kwɔːtəz] — Hauptstelle, Zentrale
to **highlight** ['haɪlaɪt] — hervorheben
to **hit a low** ['hɪt ə 'ləʊ] — einen Tiefstand erreichen
to **hold** [həʊld] — halten
honest ['ɒnɪst] — ehrlich
however [haʊ'evə] — doch, jedoch, aber, dennoch
HR (Human Resources) [,hjuːmən rɪ'sɔːsɪz] — Personal(abteilung)

I

impatient [ɪm'peɪʃnt] — ungeduldig
impressed with, be ~ [ɪm'prest wɪð] — beeindruckt sein von
to **improve** [ɪm'pruːv] — (sich) verbessern
in addition to [ɪn ə'dɪʃn tə] — zusätzlich (zu)
in charge of, to be ~ [bi ɪn 'tʃɑːdʒ əv] — verantwortlich sein für
in line with, to be ~ [ɪn 'laɪn wɪð] — Übereinstimmungen
income ['ɪnkʌm] — Einkommen
to **increase** [ɪn'kriːs] — steigen
insurance [ɪn'ʃʊərəns] — Versicherung
to **interrupt** [,ɪntə'rʌpt] — unterbrechen, ins Wort fallen
interruption [,ɪntə'rʌpʃn] — Unterbrechung, Störung
to **introduce oneself** [,ɪntrə'djuːs wʌnself] — (sich) vorstellen
investment [ɪn'vestmənt] — Investition
involved in, to be ~ [bi ɪn'vɒlvd ɪn] — beteiligt sein an
issue ['ɪʃuː] — aktuelle Frage, Thema
item ['aɪtəm] — Artikel

JK

to **join** [dʒɔɪn] — beitreten
joint venture [,dʒɔɪnt 'ventʃə] — Gemeinschaftsunternehmen
just over [dʒʌst 'əʊvə] — etwas über
just under [dʒʌst 'ʌndə] — knapp unter
to **keep calm** [kiːp 'kɑːm] — ruhig bleiben
to **know sth off the top of your head** [nəʊ ɒf ðə ,tɒp əv jɔː 'hed] — einfallen, etw spontan wissen

L

labour costs ['leɪbə kɒsts] — Personalkosten
to **launch** [lɔːntʃ] — auf den Markt bringen
to **lead to** ['liːd tə] — führen zu
to **lean forward** [liːn 'fɔːwəd] — sich nach vorne lehnen
limited contract [,lɪmɪtɪd 'kɒntrækt] — befristeter Vertrag
(line) graph ['laɪn grɑːf] — Kurvendiagramm
living expenses [lɪvɪŋ ɪk'spensɪz] — Lebenshaltungskosten

M

magnetic strip [mæg,netɪk 'strɪp] — Magnetstreifen
main part ['meɪn ,pɑːt] — Hauptteil
major ['meɪdʒə] — Haupt-, wichtig
to **make a good impression** [, meɪk ə gʊd ɪm'preʃn] — einen guten Eindruck machen
to **make sth up** [,meɪk 'ʌp] — sich etw ausdenken
to **make sure** [,meɪk 'ʃʊə] — sich vergewissern
to **manage to** ['mænɪdʒ] — gelingen (etw zu tun), (es) schaffen
marker ['mɑːkə] — Markierstift
market share ['mɑːkɪt 'ʃeə] — Marktanteil

medium-sized ['miːdiəmsaɪzd] — mittelgroß
to **meet a deadline** [miːt ə 'dedlaɪn] — einen Termin einhalten
to **mention** ['menʃn] — erwähnen
merger ['mɜːdʒə] — Fusion
microphone ['maɪkrəfəʊn] — Mikrophon
to **mind** [maɪnd] — etw dagegen haben
to **miss an opportunity** [,mɪs ən ɒpə'tjuːnəti] — eine Gelegenheit verpassen
moderately ['mɒdərətli] — gemäßigt, mäßig
monitoring equipment [,mɒnɪtərɪŋ ɪ'kwɪpmənt] — Überwachungsgeräte
motorist ['məʊtərɪst] — Autofahrer/in
to **move on to** [,muːv 'ɒn] — fortfahren, weiter gehen

N

nevertheless [,nevəðə'les] — trotzdem, dennoch
no-frills airline [nəʊ ,frɪls 'eəlaɪn] — Billigfluglinie
noisy ['nɔɪzi] — laut
to **notice** ['nəʊtɪs] — (be)merken
nursing home ['nɜːsɪŋ həʊm] — Pflegeheim

O

OHP (overhead projector) [,əʊvəhed prə'dʒektə] — Overhead-, Tageslichtprojektor
on the other hand [ɒn ði 'ʌðə hænd] — andererseits
on the right track, to be ~ [ɒn ðə ,raɪt 'træk] — auf dem richtigen Weg sein
open-plan office [,əʊpənplæn 'ɒfɪs] — Großraumbüro
order placement ['ɔːdə pleɪsmənt] — Auftragseingang
organigram [ɔː'gænɪgræm] — Organigramm
output ['aʊtpʊt] — Ausstoß, Menge
to **outsource** ['aʊtsɔːs] — auslagern, outsourcen
to **overdo sth** [,əʊvə'duː] — etw übertreiben
overhead ['əʊvəhed] — OHP-Folie
overkill ['əʊvəkɪl] — zu viel des Guten, Overkill
to **overload** [,əʊvə'ləʊd] — überladen
overseas [,əʊvə'siːz] — Ausland, Übersee
overuse [,əʊvə'juːs] — zu intensiver Gebrauch
overview ['əʊvəvjuː] — Überblick, -sicht

P

packaging ['pækɪdʒɪŋ] — Verpackung
participant [pɑː'tɪsɪpənt] — Teilnehmer/in
particularly [pə'tɪkjələli] — besonders
part-time employee [,pɑːttaɪm ɪm'plɔɪiː] — Teilzeitkraft
to **pass on** [,pɑːs 'ɒn] — weiterreichen
to **pass out** [,pɑːs 'aʊt] — austeilen, ausgeben
permission [pə'mɪʃn] — Erlaubnis, Genehmigung
to **pick up** [,pɪk 'ʌp] — zunehmen
pie chart ['paɪ tʃɑːt] — Tortendiagramm
pin board ['pɪn bɔːd] — Pinnwand
to **plant sth in sb's mind** [plɑːnt ,sʌmθɪŋ ɪn ,sʌmbədiz 'maɪnd] — etwas in jds Bewusstsein verankern
plant [plɑːnt] — Werk, Betrieb(sanlage)
to **plunge** [plʌndʒ] — abstürzen, absacken
to **point out** [,pɔɪnt 'aʊt] — hinweisen auf
pointer ['pɔɪntə] — Zeiger
to **postpone** [pə'spəʊn] — verschieben
precisely [prɪ'saɪsli] — genau
to **predict** [prɪ'dɪkt] — vorhersagen
premises ['premɪsɪz] — Geschäftsräume
prescription drugs [prɪ'skrɪpʃn drʌgz] — rezeptpflichtige Arzneimittel
present ['preznt] — gegenwärtig
to **present** [prɪ'zent] — präsentieren
to **prevent** [prɪ'vent] — (ver)hindern
previously ['priːvɪəsli] — zuvor
procedure [prə'siːdʒə] — Verfahren
progress ['prəʊgres] — Fortschritt/e
to **propose** [prə'pəʊz] — vorschlagen
proposed [prə'pəʊzd] — vorgeschlagen, geplant

pros and cons [ˌprəʊz ənd ˈkɒnz]   Für und Wider
to **prove** [pruːv]   beweisen, belegen
to **provide sb with** [prəˈvaɪd wɪð]   jdn mit etw versorgen
purpose [ˈpɜːpəs]   Zweck, Absicht
put sth into practice   etwas in die Tat/Praxis umsetzen
[ˌpʊt ɪntu ˈpræktɪs]

Q R   **quarter** [ˈkwɔːtə]   Quartal
question and answer session   Fragerunde
[kwestʃən ənd ˈɑːnsə seʃn]
R&D (Research and Development)   Forschung und Entwicklung
[rɪˌsɜːtʃ ən dɪˈveləpmənt]
rack [ræk]   Träger
to **raise sth** [reɪz]   etw erhöhen
to **raise your voice** [ˌreɪz jɔː ˈvɔɪs]   lauter sprechen
rapport [ræˈpɔː]   (enges) Verhältnis, Beziehung
rating [ˈreɪtɪŋ]   Quote
to **reach** [riːtʃ]   erreichen
to **recap** [ˈriːkæp]   (kurz) zusammenfassen
record high [ˈrekɔːd haɪ]   Rekordhöhe, Höchststand
to **recover** [rɪˈkʌvə]   sich erholen
to **recruit** [rɪˈkruːt]   (Personal) einstellen
to **reduce** [rɪˈdjuːs]   senken
to **relocate to** [ˌriːləʊˈkeɪt]   verlegen nach
to **rely on sb** [rɪˈlaɪ ɒn]   sich auf jdn verlassen
to **remain** [rɪˈmeɪn]   (ver)bleiben
remarkable [rɪˈmɑːkəbl]   bemerkenswert, beachtlich
to **remind** [rɪˈmaɪnd]   (jdn an etw) erinnern
to **replace** [rɪˈpleɪs]   ersetzen, austauschen
reputation [ˌrepjuˈteɪʃn]   Ruf
to **require** [rɪˈkwaɪə]   erforderlich machen
revenue [ˈrevənjuː]   Einkünfte, Einnahmen
to **review** [rɪˈvjuː]   zusammenfassen, einen Überblick geben
rhetorical question   rhetorische Frage
[rɪˌtɒrɪkl ˈkwestʃən]
to **rise** [raɪz]   (auf)steigen
road sign [ˈrəʊd saɪn]   Verkehrszeichen
to **rocket** [ˈrɒkɪt]   in die Höhe schnellen
roughly [ˈrʌfli]   ungefähr, etwa
round-the-clock [raʊnd ðə ˈklɒk]   rund um die Uhr
row [rəʊ]   Reihe
rude [ruːd]   unhöflich
to **run into trouble**   Schwierigkeiten bekommen
[ˌrʌn ɪntu ˈtrʌbl]
to **run through** [ˌrʌn ˈθruː]   durchgehen , überfliegen

S   **sales force** [ˈseɪlz fɔːs]   Verkaufspersonal
satisfied with sth, to be ~   zufrieden sein mit
[bi ˈsætɪsfaɪd wɪð]
schedule, tight ~ [taɪt ˈʃedjuːl]   enger Zeitplan
screen [skriːn]   Leinwand
to **set up** [ˌset ˈʌp]   aufbauen, gründen
setback [ˈsetbæk]   Rückschlag
set-up [ˈsetʌp]   Aufbau
to **share** [ʃeə]   teilen, gemeinsam nutzen
shelving system [ˈʃelvɪŋ sɪstəm]   Regalsystem
significance [sɪɡˈnɪfɪkəns]   Bedeutung
to **simplify** [ˈsɪmplɪfaɪ]   vereinfachen
sketch [sketʃ]   Skizze
ski rack [ˈskiː ræk]   Skiträger
slide [slaɪd]   (Präsentations)Folie
to **slow down your pace**   das Tempo verlangsamen
[ˌsləʊ daʊn jɔː ˈpeɪs]
to **slump** [slʌmp]   sinken, stürzen
solution [səˈluːʃn]   Lösung
to **solve** [sɒlv]   lösen
spare parts [speə ˈpɑːts]   Ersatzteile
special needs school   Sonderschule
[ˌspeʃl ˈniːdz skuːl]

to **spread** [spred]   verbreiten, verteilen
to **stand at** [ˈstænd ət]   liegen bei, stehen bei
state-of-the-art [ˌsteɪt əv ði ˈɑːt]   auf dem letzten Stand der Technik, hochmodern
steadily [ˈstedɪli]   stetig
step [step]   Schritt
to **stick to** [ˈstɪk tə]   sich richten nach
to **store** [stɔː]   lagern
straight [streɪt]   aufrecht
to **strengthen** [ˈstreŋθn]   stärken
to **stress** [stres]   betonen
to **stretch** [stretʃ]   sich strecken, dehnen
subsidiary [səbˈsɪdiəri]   Tochter(gesellschaft)
to **suit** [suːt]   passen
to **sum up** [ˌsʌm ˈʌp]   zusammenfassen
to **summarize** [ˈsʌməraɪz]   zusammenfassen
supplier [səˈplaɪə]   Lieferant, Zulieferer
support [səˈpɔːt]   Unterstützung
to **suppose** [səˈpəʊz]   annehmen
surprisingly [səˈpraɪzɪŋli]   überraschenderweise

T   **table** [ˈteɪbl]   Tabelle
to **tackle** [ˈtækl]   angehen, in Angriff nehmen
to **take care of** [teɪk ˈkeər əv]   sich kümmern um
taken over by, to be ~   übernommen werden von
[ˌteɪkən ˈəʊvə bi]
takeover [ˈteɪkəʊvə]   Übernahme
target [ˈtɑːɡɪt]   Ziel, Zielvorgabe
to **tease** [tiːz]   reizen
technical drawing [ˌteknɪkl ˈdrɔːɪŋ]   technische Zeichnung
to **tend to** [ˈtend tə]   neigen zu, tendieren zu
term [tɜːm]   Begriff, Fachwort
terms of payment   Zahlungsbedingungen
[ˌtɜːmz əv ˈpeɪmənt]
tied to, to be ~ [ˈtaɪd tə]   gebunden sein an
time frame [ˈtaɪm freɪm]   Zeitrahmen
time-consuming [ˈtaɪmkənsjuːmɪŋ]   zeitraubend
traffic [ˈtræfɪk]   (Straßen-)Verkehr
transmission [trænsˈmɪʃn]   Übertragung
transparency [trænsˈpærənsi]   Präsentationsfolie
to **treat** [triːt]   behandeln
trial run [ˈtraɪəl rʌn]   Testlauf
turnover [ˈtɜːnəʊvə]   Umsatz

U   to **underline** [ˌʌndəˈlaɪn]   unterstreichen
under-staffed [ˌʌndəˈstɑːft]   unterbesetzt
uneven [ʌnˈiːvn]   unregelmäßig, ungleichmäßig
unique [juˈniːk]   einzigartig
up to sb, to be ~ [ˌʌp tə ˈjuː, bi]   an/bei jdm liegen, (Entscheidung)
upgrade [ˌʌpˈɡreɪd]   erweitern, ausbauen, verbessern
user rights [ˈjuːzə raɪts]   Nutzungsrechte
user-friendly [juːzəˈfrendli]   benutzerfreundlich

V   **valid** [ˈvælɪd]   berechtigt
variable [ˈveəriəbl]   beweglich
varied [ˈveərid]   abwechslungsreich
various [ˈveəriəs]   verschiedene(r)
vehicle [ˈviːəkl]   Fahrzeug
viable [ˈvaɪəbl]   rentabel
video data projector   Beamer
[ˌvɪdiəʊ deɪtə prəˈdʒektə]

W   to **wave** [weɪv]   wedeln
well over [wel ˈəʊvə]   weit über
whatever [wɒtˈevə]   was auch immer
whiteboard [ˈwaɪtbɔːd]   Kunststofftafel
with regards to [wɪð rɪˈɡɑːdz tə]   in Bezug auf, bezüglich
with respect to [wɪð rɪˈspekt tə]   in Bezug auf, bezüglich
works council [ˌwɜːks ˈkaʊnsl]   Betriebsrat

Presentation trainer

Checklist – Organization

Date & time: _____

Length of time for talk: _____

Questions at end? If yes, length of time for questions: _____

Place / Room: _____

Room set-up:

Equipment needed: _____

Is it available? ☐   Does it work? ☐

Audience

	1–5	6–15	16–30	over 30
Number of people				
How much do they know about the topic?	nothing	a bit	a lot	
How well do I know them?	not at all	a little	quite well	
How formal?	very formal	formal	informal	
Nationality / Culture?	same as me	international		

Handouts   no ☐

   yes / before talk ☐   at end of talk ☐   later (intranet / email) ☐

Checklist – Contents

Topic: _____

Three main points

   1 _____

   2 _____

   3 _____

Purpose of talk: (What do I want to do?)

☐ Inform the audience

☐ Train the audience

☐ Sell something to the audience

☐ Persuade the audience to do something

Importance to audience: _____

What do I want audience to know by the end of talk: _____

Preparing visuals

How many visuals will I have? _____

Do they say (or show) what I want to say?   ☐

Are they clear and simple to understand?   ☐

Will the audience be able to read them (font size and colours)?   ☐

Do they have effective headlines?   ☐

Is there as little text as possible?   ☐

Have I remembered the rule of six?   ☐

Introduction

Welcome audience.

_____

_____

_____

Introduce yourself (name, position/function).

_____

_____

_____

State your topic.

_____

_____

_____

Say why your topic is important for the audience.

_____

_____

_____

Describe the structure of your talk (the main points and when you will be dealing with them).

_____

_____

_____

_____

_____

_____

Say how long the talk will be.

_____

_____

Say when you will answer questions.

_____

_____

Say whether there are handouts.

_____

_____

> **TIP**
> Remember how to make effective openings: start with a rhetorical question, a story or an amazing fact, or give the audience a problem to think about.

Main part

Briefly state your topic and objective(s) again.

_____

_____

_____

_____

Then introduce your three (or two or ?) main points and give details.

Main point 1:

_____

_____

_____

_____

_____

_____

Main point 2:

_____

_____

_____

_____

_____

_____

Main point 3:

_____

_____

_____

_____

_____

Signal the end of the main part.

_____

_____

_____

_____

REMEMBER TO:
- signal the beginning of each part.
- talk about your topic.
- signal the end of each part.
- highlight the main points.
- summarize the main ideas.

BULLET CHARTS?
- Refer to points in the same order.
- Use the same key words and phrases as on your bullet charts.

GRAPHS, TABLES, PIE CHARTS, ETC?
- Start by telling your audience what the visual illustrates.
- Explain it if necessary.
- Highlight the key points.
- Say why these points are important (and explain the cause or effect).

Conclusion

Signal the end of your talk

_____

_____

Summarize the key points

_____

_____

Highlight one important point

_____

_____

Explain the significance

_____

_____

Make your final statement

_____

_____

Invite questions

_____

Dealing with questions

What questions can I expect?	How can I answer them?
1	
2	
3	
4	
5	
6	
7	
8	

TIP

Remember how to make effective conclusions: end with a question or a quote from a famous person, finish a story you started at the beginning of your talk or call the audience to action.

TIP

Remember, when answering questions during or after your talk:
- Listen carefully and make sure you have understood the question correctly.
- Reformulate the question if necessary.
- If you want to postpone the question, say why politely.
- If you don't know the answer, say so and offer to find out.
- Answer irrelevant questions politely but briefly.
- Check that the questioner is satisfied with your answer.

Checklist – Feedback

Organization

Was my presentation the right length?
too long ☐   too short ☐   just right ☐
Was there time for questions at the end (if relevant)?
too long ☐   too short ☐   just right ☐

TIP

Use this checklist after a practice talk or an actual talk to evaluate your own performance!

Communication

How was my body language?
good ☐   bad ☐   Why?_____

How well did I deal with nervousness?
well ☐   not well ☐   Why? _____

Did the audience understand me?
yes, all the time ☐   yes, most of the time ☐   yes, some of the time ☐   no ☐

Did I have trouble expressing myself in English?
yes, all the time ☐   yes, most of the time ☐   yes, some of the time ☐   no ☐

What were some words or phrases I needed but didn't know?

_____

Look them up!

Parts of the presentation

Introduction   Did I tell the audience the purpose of my talk?   yes ☐   no ☐
Did I explain the structure of my talk?   yes ☐   no ☐
Did I tell the audience why the talk was relevant to them?   yes ☐   no ☐

• How can I improve the introduction? _____

Main part   Did I state my main points clearly?   yes ☐   no ☐
Did I use effective signposting?   yes ☐   no ☐
Did I emphasize key points?   yes ☐   no ☐
Did I summarize key points after each section?   yes ☐   no ☐
Did I present my visuals well?   yes ☐   no ☐

• How can I improve the main part? _____

Conclusion   Did I summarize the key points?   yes ☐   no ☐
Did I tell the audience what to do (call to action)?   yes ☐   no ☐
Did I leave a lasting impression?   yes ☐   no ☐

• How can I improve the conclusion? _____

Questions   How well did I deal with questions?   very well ☐   well ☐   fairly well ☐   badly ☐
• Why? _____
• What questions were asked that I didn't anticipate? _____

• How can I improve the way I deal with questions? _____

Useful phrases and vocabulary

INTRODUCTION

Welcoming the audience
Good morning/afternoon, ladies and gentlemen.
Hello/Hi everyone.
First of all, let me thank you all for coming here today.
It's a pleasure to welcome you today.
I'm happy/delighted that so many of you could make it today.
It's good to see you all here.

Introducing yourself
Let me introduce myself. I'm Ann Brown from ...
For those of you who don't know me, my name is ...
Let me just start by introducing myself. My name is ...

Giving your position, function, department, company
As some of you know, I'm the purchasing manager.
I'm the key account manager here and am responsible for ...
I'm here in my function as the head of ...
I'm the project manager in charge of ...

Introducing your topic
What I'd like to present to you today is ...
I'm here today to present ...
Today's topic is ...
The subject/topic of my presentation is ...
In my presentation I would like to report on ...
In my talk I'll tell you about ...
Today I'm going to talk about ...
I'll be talking about ...

Saying why your topic is relevant for your audience
Today's topic is of particular interest to those of you/us who ...
My talk is particularly relevant to those of us who ...
My topic is/will be very important for you because ...
By the end of this talk you will be familiar with ...

Stating your purpose
The purpose/objective/aim of this presentation is to ...
Our goal is to determine how/the best way to ...
What I want to show you is ...
My objective is to ...
Today I'd like to give you an overview of ...
Today I'll be showing you/reporting on ...
I'd like to update you on/inform you about ...
During the next few hours we'll be ...

Structuring
I've divided my presentation into three (main) parts.
In my presentation I'll focus on three major issues.

Sequencing
Point one deals with ..., point two ..., and point three ...
First, I'll be looking at ..., second ..., and third ...
I'll begin/start off by .... Then I'll move on to ...
    Then/Next/After that ...
I'll end with ...

Timing
My presentation will take about 30 minutes.
It will take about 20 minutes to cover these issues.
This won't take more than ...

Handouts
Does everybody have a handout/brochure/copy of the report? Please take one and pass them on.
Don't worry about taking notes. I've put all the important statistics on a handout for you.
I'll be handing out copies of the slides at the end of my talk.
I can email the PowerPoint presentation to anybody who wants it.

Questions
There will be time for questions after my presentation.
We will have about 10 minutes for questions in the question and answer period.
If you have any questions, feel free to interrupt me at any time.
Feel free to ask questions at any time during my talk.

EFFECTIVE OPENINGS

Rhetorical questions
Is market research important for brand development?
Do we really need quality assurance?

Interesting facts
According to an article I read recently, ...
Did you know that ... ?
I'd like to share an amazing fact/figure with you.

Stories and anecdotes
I remember when I attended a meeting in Paris, ...
At a conference in Madrid, I was once asked the following question: ...
Let me tell you what happened to me ...

Problem to think about
Suppose you wanted to ... . How would you go about it?
Imagine you had to ... . What would be your first step?

THE MIDDLE/MAIN PART

Saying what is coming
In this part of my presentation, I'd like to talk about ...
So, let me first give you a brief overview.

Indicating the end of a section
This brings me to the end of my first point.
So much for point two.
So, that's the background on ...
That's all I wanted to say about ...

Summarizing a point
Before I move on, I'd like to recap the main points.
Let me briefly summarize the main issues.
I'd like to summarize what I've said so far ...

Moving to the next point
This leads directly to my next point.
This brings us to the next question.
Let's now move on/turn to ...
After examining this point, let's turn to ...
Let's now take a look at ...

Going back
As I said/mentioned earlier, ...
Let me come back to what I said before ...
Let's go back to what we were discussing earlier.
As I've already explained, ...
As I pointed out in the first section, ...

Referring to other points
I have a question in connection with/concerning payment.
There are a few problems regarding the quality.
With respect/regard to planning, we need more background information.
According to the survey, our customer service needs reviewing.

Adding ideas
In addition to this, I'd like to say that our IT business is going very well.
Moreover/Furthermore, there are other interesting facts we should take a look at.
Apart from being too expensive, this model is too big.

Talking about (difficult) issues
I think we first need to identify the problem.
Of course we'll have to clarify a few points before we start.
We will have to deal with the problem of increasing prices.
How shall we cope with unfair business practices?
The question is: why don't we tackle the distribution problems?
If we don't solve this problem now, we'll get/run into serious trouble soon.
We will have to take care of this problem now.
We are currently having difficulties with ...

Rhetorical questions
What conclusion can we draw from this?
So, what does this mean?
So, just how good are the results?
So, how are we going to deal with this increase?

So, where do we go from here?
Why do I say that? Because ...
Do we really want to miss this opportunity to ...?

DESCRIBING VISUALS

Introducing a visual
Let's now look at the next slide which shows ...
To illustrate this, let's have a closer look at ...
The chart on the following slide shows ...
I have a slide here that shows ...
The problem is illustrated in the next bar chart ...
According to this graph, our net profit has doubled.
You can see the test results in this table.
As you can see here, ...

Explaining a visual
First, let me quickly explain the graph.
You can see that different colours have been used to indicate ...
The new models are listed across the bottom.
The biggest segment indicates ...
The key in the bottom left-hand corner ...

Highlighting information
I'd like to stress/highlight/emphasize the following point(s).
I'd like to start by drawing your attention to ...
Let me point out that ...
I think you'll be surprised to see that ...
I'd like you to focus your attention on ...
What's really important here is ...
What I'd like to point out here is ...
Let's look more closely at ...

Describing trends
Sales increased slightly in summer.
Consumer spending fell/declined sharply.
Interest rates have risen steadily.
Food prices went up significantly.
There was a sudden increase in prices.
In August, we saw a moderate fall.
This was followed by a gradual decline.
There was a sharp slump in sales.
Ticket sales have started picking up.

Explaining purpose
We introduced this method to increase flexibility.
The purpose of this step is to expand to foreign markets.
Our aim was to ...

Explaining cause and effect
What's the reason for this drastic decrease?
The unexpected drop was caused by ...
This was because of ...
As a consequence/Consequently, sales went up significantly.
As a result ...
The venture resulted in a sharp fall in share prices.
Our new strategy has led to an increase of 10%.

CONCLUSION

Indicating the end of your talk
I'm now approaching/nearing the end of my presentation.
Well, this brings me to the end of my presentation.
That covers just about everything I wanted to say about …
OK, I think that's everything I wanted to say about …
As a final point, I'd like to …
Finally, I'd like to highlight one key issue.

Summarizing points
Before I stop, let me go over the key issues again.
Just to summarize the main points of my talk …
I'd like to run through my main points again …
To conclude/In conclusion, I'd like to …
To sum up (then), we …

Making recommendations
We'd suggest …
We therefore (strongly) recommend that …
In my opinion, we should …
Based on the figures we have, I'm quite certain that …

Inviting questions
Are there any questions?
We just have time for a few questions.
And now I'll be happy to answer any questions you may have.

EFFECTIVE CONCLUSIONS

Quoting a well-known person
As … once said, …
To quote a well-known businessman, …
To put it in the words of …

Referring back to the beginning
Remember what I said at the beginning of my talk today?
Let me just go back to the story I told you earlier. Remember, …

DEALING WITH QUESTIONS

Clarifying questions
I'm afraid I didn't (quite) catch that.
I'm sorry, could you repeat your question, please?
So, if I understood you correctly, you would like to know whether …
So, in other words you would like to know whether …
If I could just rephrase your question. You'd like to know …
Does that answer your question?

Avoiding giving an answer
If you don't mind, could we discuss that on another occasion?
I'm afraid that's not really what we're discussing today.
Well, actually I'd prefer not to discuss that today.

Admitting you don't know
Sorry, I don't know that off the top of my head.
I'm afraid I'm not in a position to answer that question at the moment.
I'm afraid I don't know the answer to your question, but I'll try to find out for you.
Sorry, that's not my field. But I'm sure Peter Bott from Sales could answer your question.

Postponing questions
If you don't mind, I'll deal with/come back to this point later in my presentation.
Can we get back to this point a bit later?
I'd prefer to answer your question in the course of my presentation.
Would you mind waiting until the question and answer session at the end?
Perhaps we could go over this after the presentation.

Summarizing after interruptions
Before we go on, let me briefly summarize the points we've discussed.
So, now I'd like to return to what we were discussing earlier.

USEFUL WORDS (IN CONTEXT)

to clarify	Before we go on, let me clarify one point.	klären
to focus on	We need to focus on customer service.	sich konzentrieren auf
to highlight	Let me highlight the following points.	hervorheben
to illustrate	This chart illustrates our success story.	darstellen
to indicate	The figures on the left indicate sales in France.	zeigen, angeben
to lead to	This leads to my next point.	führen zu
to mention	As I mentioned earlier, our staff is well-qualified.	erwähnen
to move on to	Let's now move on to the next question.	weiter gehen
to note	Please note that prices rose slightly.	beachten
to notice	You'll notice a sharp drop in August.	bemerken
to pass on	Here are the handouts. Please take one and pass them on.	weiterreichen
to rise	House prices rose by 5% last year.	steigen
to solve	How can we solve this problem?	lösen
to summarize	Before I go on, let me summarize the key issues.	zusammenfassen
to update	I'd like to update you on the project status.	auf den neusten Stand bringen